EVER LIGHT AND DARK

TELLING SECRETS, TELLING THE TRUTH

ELIZABETH MILLER HAYES

CONTENTS

PRAISE FOR EVER LIGHT
AND DARK

Elizabeth's invitation is winsome, approachable, honest, and lovely. She hands you her life, simply and directly, and lets you conclude what you will. It's a refreshing freedom.

Matthew Tiemeyer

Licensed Mental Health Counselor, Blue Harbor Counseling

Elizabeth believes our stories are a doorway to know God. This book will awaken your heart to your own stories and to the heartache that calls us to seek a larger story. She invites us to engage in the wonder and redemption of our darkest moments. You will be in awe of your own life, and even more in awe of the God who wrote your life.

Becky Allender

Author, *Hidden in Plain Sight*

The past is a complicated thing, and Elizabeth leaves it that way. But in leaving it so, she leaves us richer for having walked through it with her. The unveiling of a life's secrets drives each page turn, but it is the things she's learned along the way—about family, God, and herself—that will bless us in each chapter of our lives.

Andrew Van Kirk
Priest, St. Andrew's Episcopal Church

There is no pretense here. All the highs, lows, and in-betweens of the human experience are contained in this book. Though heart-wrenching at times, her story brims with gentleness, laughter, and astonishing forgiveness. Driven to the feet of Christ, Elizabeth discovers that he'd been pursuing her all along.

Katie Hautamaki
Event Director, MidTown Reader
Former Editor, *New York Family Magazine*

Like an anticipated college roommate reunion over a bottle of Bordeaux, the honest dialogue in this book flows freely. There is comfort and safety, and like words from a good friend, needed truth that is sometimes painful to hear. By book's end, you'll be renewed from the visit and redirected in your focus. Welcome home readers . . . your search for connection is over!

Patricia E. Grisso
Licensed Marriage and Family Therapist

Elizabeth Miller Hayes' *Ever Light and Dark* is a beautiful and important book. It is a journey into the story of a life—hers, and one that leaves readers with the challenge to reflect on God's unfailing pursuit in their own stories. I love that Elizabeth refuses to with-hold the raw and sometimes painful details of her personal strug-gles, and thus offers hope that God can take the broken pieces of any journey and redeem them into something beautiful.

Mike Khandjian
Pastor, Chapelgate Presbyterian Church
Author, *A Sometimes Stumbling Life*

At times you'll ache reading the memorable snapshots of Elizabeth's life. Ultimately, you'll appreciate the honest, persistent, soul-searching that evolves into remarkable life-lessons. This book is filled with hope, acceptance, and forgiveness.

Marilyn Morris

Founder, Aim for Success, Inc.

The Apostle Paul said when he was weak, he was strong. In sharing her pain and her experiences of how God brought healing, Elizabeth has allowed the Lord to use her powerfully in all of our lives. Her precious encouragement reminds us we are not alone.

Chuck Ryor

Pastor, Prism Church

Elizabeth writes with authenticity and steers clear of platitudes and clichés. She stands honestly in her own story, and her courage inspires me to do the same.

Shannan McEowen,

Ministry Coordinator, Chase Oaks Church

Published by White Blackbird Books, an imprint of Storied Publishing

Copyright ©2019 by Elizabeth Miller Hayes

Permission requests and other questions may be directed to the Contact page at www.storied.pub.

Unless otherwise indicated, Scripture quotations are from the ESV Bible (The Holy Bible, English Standard Version), copyright 2001 by Crossway, a publishing ministry of Good News Publishers. 2011 Text Edition. All rights reserved.

Printed in the USA

ISBN-13:9781733592109

Cover art by Beth Marie Meggs

Cover layout by Sean Benesh

Edited by Claire Berger and Julie Serven

ABOUT WHITE BLACKBIRD BOOKS

White blackbirds are extremely rare, but they are real. They are blackbirds that have turned white over the years as their feathers have come in and out over and over again. They are a redemptive picture of something you would never expect to see but that has slowly come into existence over time.

There is plenty of hurt and brokenness in the world. There is the hopelessness that comes in the midst of lost jobs, lost health, lost homes, lost marriages, lost children, lost parents, lost dreams, loss.

But there also are many white blackbirds. There are healed marriages, children who come home, friends who are reconciled. There are hurts healed, children fostered and adopted, communities restored. Some would call these events entirely natural, but really they are unexpected miracles.

The books in this series are not commentaries, nor are they crammed with unique insights. Rather, they are a collage of biblical truth applied to current times and places. The authors share their poverty and trust the Lord to use their words to strengthen and encourage his people.

May this series help you in your quest to know Christ as he is found in the Gospel through the Scriptures. May you look for and even expect the rare white blackbirds of God's redemption through Christ in your midst. May you be thankful when you look down and see your feathers have turned. May you also rejoice when you see that others have been unexpectedly transformed by Jesus.

For my mother and sisters.
And for all those who mothered and sistered me.

Your lives and your stories, told and untold, matter.
Your pain is not forgotten.

WHO AM I?

I am not an afterthought, an accident, or a problem I must fix.

I was created, I was chosen, and I am loved.

I have light and joy and beauty and humor.

I also have darkness and grief and fear.

I am shortsighted and anxious and self-centered.

I am also hopeful and calm and thoughtful.

I worry, *and* I pray.

I am present, and I regularly choose to escape.

I know how to survive and endure.

I am learning how to thrive and take risks.

I take responsibility for my choices.

I start over every day, sometimes multiple times a day.

I am a seeker of things that are true.

I like to share those things when I find them.

I am real and genuinely open.

I sometimes like to hide by silencing myself.

I am learning that when I do that, I am hiding light.

I long to be seen.

I feel both young and old, frequently throughout the same day.

I matter simply because I am created.

I don't need to constantly prove my right to exist by producing.

I know how to love, although imperfectly.

I know how to withhold love, and everyone suffers when I do, especially me.

I am loved, I am.

I am not my body.

I am not what I do.

I am a child, a woman, a lover, a friend, a wife, a mother, a student, and a teacher.

I am a soul.

My soul has a voice . . . and I intend to use it.

INTRODUCTION

This book isn't for everyone. It contains stories from my life, and I share them not because I am a wise guru, but because they are truthful and real. This is *not* a self-help book or a Christian living manual in disguise. Living in reality and awareness with room for faith has become my greatest passion. Real life as I know it is a strange and often unwanted mixture of joy and pain. When I accept this, I start to actually feel my life.

I am a walking paradox, a person of faith and a person of doubt. I believe God loves me, but have trouble feeling it sometimes. I experience sublimely sacred moments, as well as intense irreverent angst—sometimes within the same twenty-four hours. I don't think this makes me a hypocrite; I think it makes me honest.

I continuously fight the urge to give in to cynicism. When I hear Christian-ese, it makes me want to bang my head against a wall. It feels forced and dishonest. I desire to live life honestly, even if I don't have all the answers.

A few decades ago, I began looking more closely at some of the pain in my life and the lingering questions that came with it. I had grown tired of the easy answers and worn-out platitudes. I set out to find a more honest way of living a life of faith. I didn't abandon all the tenets of Christianity; in fact, some became even more precious to me. But it's not the religion I grew up with. It's more nuanced than that. There's more mystery and often more questions than answers. But the most important thing it is, is real. I am often surprised as I experience a God who refuses to be controlled or reduced to a formula for successful living. God doesn't promise the elimination of suffering, only that he will be with us in it. Christ seems to love a good story too and often responds to people with stories rather than direct answers. He also seems to offer himself rather than formulas or prescriptive methods. So I want to try to do the same: to offer some stories and myself. My desire is that they will strengthen your hope, even in darkness.

DARKNESS DESCENDS

1

CAREFREE SUNNY DAYS

Every person has a moment in life when perception is shattered and life changes forever. Something so signifi-cant happens that he or she can never go back to seeing life the same way as before. Some call this the breaking of *shalom*, or peace. It can occur when someone is a child, teenager, or adult. It can be something as severe as child abuse or less drastic, like being made fun of by classmates or rejected by the opposite sex for the first time.

Whatever the event, it is devastating to the person who experi-ences it. Awakening to the reality of brokenness in the world, in the people around us and in ourselves, is an unwanted clarity most of us would much rather avoid.

My awakening came when I was three years old and realized for the first time that my father was gone. I didn't understand divorce, how far Florida was from California, or why I wouldn't see my father again for four years. I was just a girl who needed her father, and he was nowhere to be found. As far as I knew, I might never see him again. Each day was now filled with intermittent tears and unanswered questions. In the most abrupt way, the sun began to fade. I would be introduced to more darkness in the coming years, but even then life wasn't always dark. I had a few years filled with carefree sunny days.

From those years, I remember a few snapshot moments. I remember swimming in a pool, sitting in a shopping cart in the grocery store with my mom, hugging/strangling the family kitten, eating cantaloupe. I don't remember my room, or my brothers or sisters, or our house. I don't remember my parents talking, laughing, arguing, crying, or even being together. I don't remember their faces or their arms holding me. I definitely don't remember their divorce, or leaving on a plane with my mother and oldest brother. I remember moments: happy, playful, seemingly insignificant moments.

As mothers sometimes do, mine tells a sentimental story of the day of my birth. The day before my thirty-fourth birthday, my mother sent me a handwritten note telling part of my birth story. I still have this sweet note in my box of favorite cards and letters. It says:

Dear Elizabeth,
This morning I remembered how I walked to the grocery store, heavy with you, and had to stop on the way back and sit on the side of the curb to rest. The next day, thirty-four years ago, I prepared to have you by washing my hair and laying your baby clothes out for your arrival. Sure enough, you were born in the afternoon. God blessed me with a beautiful baby girl. I think of this every April 1st . . . for me, the first day of spring, and I give thanks to God for the springtime and for you. I love you.
–Mom

I was the fourth child to enter our family, in 1970. I am told I was a smiley baby and toddler—open and affectionate. I trusted everyone, was curious about everything, and was fearless. I lived with my mother, father, two older brothers, and one older sister. I was content—the quality I miss most now.

Life changed drastically when my parents divorced. My mother, oldest brother Bryan, and I soon moved from our home in Miami to the tiny town of Anza, California, in the mountains above San Diego. We lived in a big white wooden house with a man named Richard, who eventually became my stepfather. Richard was a good bit older than my mother, about seventeen years. He seemed more like a strange old person living in my mother's room. I remember going into her room once without knocking and seeing Richard come out of the bathroom in large, white underwear. I definitely never went into her room again without knocking.

Richard was an eccentric nutritionist who always carried a toothbrush in his shirt pocket with the head of it wrapped in a napkin. He barely spoke to me and was good at occupying himself wherever I was not. I don't remember ever receiving a kind look or word from him. He didn't yell at me or hit me; he simply tolerated me when he was there. He traveled a lot, which I think was fine with my mother, brother, and me.

I was generally happy in Anza, a small town of about 5,000, with houses spread out on acres and small roads connecting them. Our house had a white gravel lane leading up to it from the main road. We had an antique water pump, painted red. There were miles of trees along either side of the road leading up to the house. I regularly played in those forests, making forts out of sticks and glass bottle lids.

The inside of the house was normal '70s décor—lots of orange and green and yellow. An olive green wall phone with a long cord wrapped around everything in its wake. The couch in the living room was near the front door, but we had no TV in that room, or any room. There was a sandbox outside, and we also had a stable with two horses, Marky and Bo. We had chickens, a couple of dogs, and what seemed like a dozen cats, although it was probably only two or three. My brother

Bryan and I had our own rooms at the top of the stairs. Bryan was seven years older than me, so even though our rooms were right across from each other, I rarely saw him. He was busy doing ten-year-old boy things. A three-year-old sister apparently was not useful or fun.

I have other random memories, like eating steamed artichokes with drawn butter at the dining room table by myself. Pretty fancy cuisine for a three-year-old, but I loved it. We never ate meals together. My mother would eat as she cooked, serve me, and I would sit by myself. My brother and Richard were never around. I don't know where they were, but family dinner wasn't something we did. My mother always fed me healthy, home-cooked meals. We never went out to eat. We also never ate junk food, sugar cereals, or pizza. I didn't even know those things existed, so I couldn't, and didn't, complain.

I was about seven before I ate a cheeseburger or drank a milk-shake. My mother took me on a trip to Palm Springs, where my stepfather Richard had another house. We went to one of those old-fashioned diners, where everything is black and white and red and you sit at the bar on those spinning high-top chairs. I had my first cheeseburger, French fries, and a chocolate shake. It was like I'd died and gone to food heaven. My taste buds exploded, and that meal would remain a symbol of childhood bliss.

The rest of the happy memories involve my room and all my favorite toys and dolls. I spent much of my time alone in my room when I wasn't playing outside. I spent hours and hours with Barbie and Ken dolls, moving them around in all the rooms of their plastic house. I had an excellent selection of Fisher Price toys, including a plastic record player that played 45s and a Sit & Spin. Everything was pink and white and lacey and girly. Sunlight poured through one wall of windows in the attic-style room. I felt safe and happy there.

It was a sweet, simple life. I knew nothing about the world, good or bad. I anticipated nothing and lived in the moment. I woke without an alarm, rolled out of bed, went to breakfast in my pajamas, and ate food prepared by someone else. I stopped eating when I was full, wandered to the television, and settled onto the couch to watch a show. After a while, I would play in my room until I was hungry for lunch and then return to the table of never-ending food. I would go outside for the afternoon and play with the animals, dig in the sandbox, stroll to the river, or make tree forts. I had no concept of time; I just knew to go home before the sun went down. Life was good then.

2

BREACH OF INNOCENCE

In my new home, Richard certainly was not a replacement father to me. He seemed to barely know I existed, and for the most part my mother made sure to keep me out of his way. I only remember Richard actually speaking to me a handful of times over a ten-year period.

When I would cry and beg for my real father, my mother would just say, "It'll be okay," which was not an answer and made me more hysterical as I wondered where he'd gone. Even now, more than forty years later, I still remember the desperate feeling in my chest, the lump in my throat, and the pain in my heart as I looked into her eyes and heard empty words. I wanted to know where my father was. I needed him. I needed to see a look of love and adoration in his eyes, to sit on his lap, to feel his hugs. . . . But he wasn't there. No one was. Until the day I found the man next door.

In a town of 5,000 people, you think you know everyone and that everyone is good and kind and can be trusted. At least that's what I assume my mother thought. Why else would she let me wander around, unsupervised, unnoticed, and unprotected? She worked at a nutrition store. Next door to the store was a realtor's office, where the man owned a business. He was often there alone, with no secretary or clients.

One day, while my mother was working and I was hanging around the store, I wandered next door to the man's office. He was sitting at his desk and smiled at me when I came in. I don't know how long I was gone, but it was long enough for something terrible to happen.

The office was one big room with wood paneling on the walls and beige carpet on the floor. His desk was to the right, and a couch and table were to the left. I was so little I could hide and play underneath the table. I was a cheerful little girl, with big eyes and long brown hair. I looked at him and smiled and giggled, the way a lot of little girls do.

I don't remember him saying anything to me. He just sat at his desk and smiled at me as he watched me play. He seemed interested, and that was enough for me. I kept playing and stayed hidden under the table, where I could still see him and he could still see me. His desk was the kind you could see underneath from across the room.

All of a sudden I saw him do something strange, something I'd never seen before. He was still sitting at his desk, but he had put his hand in his lap. He was holding something in it. I didn't know what it was but it made me feel funny and I began to get uncomfortable. He started doing something a person could be arrested for if caught in public, and all the while he was still smiling at me. I felt nervous and my stomach felt sick. Something was happening to me physiologically, as my four-year-old mind could not process what I was seeing. It felt like electricity, or heat, in my lungs and stomach. I didn't know what was happening, but I didn't run away yet. I kept nervously smiling and giggling. He never got up from the desk while he was engaged in the illegal act. He never came over to me or touched me or spoke to me. He just kept smiling. His smile confused me even more.

I eventually scurried back to my mother's store. I was in a daze and disoriented. Still, my attention span was the length of most children that age, and I quickly forgot what I saw, what the man was doing, and went back to playing in a new spot. I don't remember my mother greeting me or even noticing I was gone. I didn't tell her what happened; I didn't know anything significant had. In fact, it did not cross my mind again for almost ten years.

I wish I could tell you that man and the secret life he lived never crossed my path again. Unfortunately, later that same year, my mother let him take me to his house for ice cream. How this even came about, I'll never know. Did my mother actually give him permission? Maybe he lied and told her he was just taking me for ice cream. Either way, it's so hard for me to understand how she could allow a virtual stranger to take me anywhere. Maybe it was what people did back then; it was the '70s, and I assume my mother thought everyone in this small town could be trusted.

I remember his white trailer in the middle of a green field. I don't remember any ice cream, any conversation, or anyone else around. He opened the door and said I could jump on the bed if I wanted. I began playing and jumping and saw he had kneeled down at the end of the bed. He never stopped smiling at me. I was rolling back and forth, being playful. All of a sudden, he began taking my clothes off. I didn't stop him; I didn't know I should have. No one ever told me this was not okay. He never touched me, but I did feel that same nervous feeling again, and I didn't know what to do.

I was four years old. I knew very little about anything that was going on in that room or in the world in general. Someone was paying attention to me. I liked and needed attention. I didn't know it was wrong. I didn't know much of anything, except that I was left alone a lot and I missed my father. Nobody wants to think about how to tell a four-year-old not to let anyone take off her clothes, but someone should have. Better yet, I never should have been alone with the man next door in the first place.

Once again, I never told my mother. As I got older and began to understand more about these kinds of things, I had memories of it happening. I felt uncomfortable, dirty, and ashamed. I didn't think I had done anything wrong; I thought something was wrong with *me*.

What was it about me that made him pick me? Was I the kind of bad girl that dirty old men were attracted to? I thought the same horrible thing you hear people say sometimes: She must have been asking for it. After all I was very playful, trusting, and friendly. It probably *was* my fault, I thought.

That's how children think who don't know any better. If a child is left too long unattended and unnoticed by the people responsible for caring for her, someone else will notice her. But it won't be the person who should.

Later, when I was about thirteen, my friend and I were hanging outside a theater at night after seeing a movie. We were young and doing stupid things, like getting kicked out of movies for laughing and talking too loud. That night, a van drove slowly by where we were standing. It was the strangest thing. The sliding door to the van was open, and a man was hanging halfway out the door. We laughed and thought little of it.

A few minutes later, that same man walked by us with his pants undone and his privates hanging out. He cornered us and tried to take advantage of us. My friend ran away, but I was so paralyzed with fear that I couldn't move. He pushed me up against the building. Fortunately, I was finally able to slip away before any greater harm was done. Again I remember thinking: What is wrong with me? Why do these strange, perverted men keep finding me? I thought it was because I was damaged and something was not right about me.

The truth was it was because I was vulnerable and unprotected. Men like this know what to look for. They know a target when they see one. They saw my vulnerability, careless manner, lack of awareness, insecurity, and my need for attention.

I carried the shame of these incidents into my teenage, college, and adult years. I believed the lie that it was my fault and that I was *that* kind of girl. This happens when we don't tell anyone secrets like these; they get bigger and darker and become something they're not. They become the lie we tell ourselves over and over about who we are and what we're worth.

I wish these things had never happened to me. I wish they never happened to anyone. I wish I could take back all those years of shame and secrets. I wish someone had been watching out for me more. But wishing doesn't make it so.

If I had a daughter, I would raise her differently. But since I don't, I can only hope that if anything like this has happened to you or someone you know, you will tell someone and start believing the truth. *The truth is it wasn't your fault, and you are worth far more than you will ever know.*

.

3

NO WAY OUT

When I was five my mother sent me to live as a boarding student with a German woman. She was supposedly a gifted teacher and au pair of sorts. My mother and I lived in San Diego. Mrs. M, the teacher, lived in Los Angeles. There were two other children who boarded with her when I was there. Mrs. M was probably in her late fifties. She lived in a small one-bedroom apartment in East LA. During the day, the three of us attended the elementary school where she taught. At night we came home to stay with her. I lived with her, if you could call it that, for two months.

She began beating the three of us almost immediately. We were told we must teach ourselves to read without any instruction. Mrs. M said we should be able to "figure it out." She would sit on the couch, tell us to line up single file with our books, and say, "Go ahead, read to me." One by one, we went up to her, tried to read, and failed. "But you haven't taught us how yet," we would say, and she would slap us on the side of our legs with a belt, one slap for every time we didn't read. She did not yell, only kept repeating herself, then hitting us. Again and again the same futile exercise:

back in line, attempt to read, fail, slap. I began to tremble and sweat as I neared the front of the line. I felt like a switch flipped inside me; I turned cold and a little numb. Still, I kept lining up. I didn't know what else to do.

One morning I woke up and noticed my thighs were black and blue. After my shower, I showed Mrs. M. "Look what happened to me," I said. She began sobbing uncontrollably, saying "I'm sorry, I'm so sorry," over and over. It seemed to me like she meant it. Her tears and her words comforted me. I even cried with her and let her hug me.

Her remorse didn't last long. Late that night, after we had eaten dinner, Mrs. M made us sit at the table and do our homework without any help. We were not allowed to get up from the table until we were finished. We sat there for hours, staring at each other and the books. Mrs. M pulled her twin bed out into the living room next to the table, so she could make sure we didn't get up. It got so late that she eventually fell asleep. Still we sat at the table, exhausted and confused. We kept nodding off. At about 2 a.m., I finally crawled down onto the floor beside the table and fell asleep. The other two kids soon followed me.

The next morning we awoke to the belt slapping us on our bare backs (we often went without shirts in the LA heat). The sound was like cracks of lightning. "I told you not to move until you completed your homework!" Mrs. M repeated as she hit us. I was terrified and disoriented. We screamed so loudly that she finally stopped. She told us to get up, stop crying, and get ready for school.

We each got the bathroom to ourselves for our daily shower. The shower was my only sanctuary; I could lock the door and be alone. I would go into what felt like a trance as the hot water washed over me, calming and settling me. A small window above the shower faced a playground with a swing set and basketball court. You couldn't see much—only a part of the sky—but you could hear children playing and laughing. I would stand in the shower staring out that window for as long as I could, until Mrs. M yelled through the door to hurry up and get out. It was the only peaceful, safe time of the day. She couldn't hurt me in there.

Every day was like being in a dream, a mix of confusion and anxiousness. Mrs. M would be nice one minute and horrid the next. Day after day the same routine: wake, shower, school, beatings. It seemed like it would never end. I felt trapped, controlled, and abandoned, although I didn't know that word at the time. I knew I was on my own. This was my introduction to powerlessness. It was the worst feeling I'd ever known. It still is.

I lived there for two months, but it seemed more like years. My mother came to visit me one month into my stay. She picked me up at the apartment and took me to a restaurant and the ballet. I was desperate to tell her what was going on. I pulled her aside in the bathroom at the restaurant, crying hysterically, trying to tell her what Mrs. M was doing. I showed her my legs as proof. But by the time of my mother's visit, most of the bruises had disappeared, and she thought I was making up a story so I could go home. The more she dismissed what I was saying, the more hysterical I became. When she finally said, "That's enough, let's go!" I lost all feeling in my body. I was crushed. She had come back for me, only to return me to hell again.

Later the next month, while Mrs. M was out of the apartment using the building's laundry facilities, I ran to the phone in the living room and tried to call someone to get me out of there. But I was only five. I didn't know how to use the phone or who to call. I didn't know my mother's number or the number for the police, so I called the operator and kept saying, "I need to get out of here! Someone please help me! I need my Mommy! I need my Mommy!" I began crying as I desperately repeated myself. Eventually I heard Mrs. M coming back, so I frantically hung up the phone and stood still. When she opened the door, all hope of rescue was gone.

I remember the feeling I had in my stomach and in my chest. My mind raced. That was my last chance to get out; no one was coming to save me now. If there's such a thing as "breaking," or dying while continuing to exist, I died that day, or at least a part of me did. For the rest of my time there, I was like a robot, going through the motions each day, one after the other, until one day it was over. The two months had ended, and my mother came to get me. I don't remember anything about that day. I wish I could say I was relieved or happy, but by then I felt nothing at all. I went home, and we never talked about it again.

I think of that time long ago as one of the defining moments of my life. I feel sorry for my five-year-old self in Mrs. M's apartment. I feel sorry for all I lost there, and I feel sorry for any child who knows what it's like to feel hope die. Especially when you are a child, you don't choose much of anything. You don't choose your parents, family, home, where you'll go to school, who will take care of you. Your choices are limited to what you want for breakfast and which doll you'll sleep with at night. The consequences of the choices someone else made for me when I was young were long-lasting.

About fifteen years after my time with Mrs. M, I discovered that she had been arrested for child abuse. I asked my mother about it to see what her response would be. When I thought back over the years, I realized I had become angry at my mother: for taking me there, for leaving me there, for not believing me. As I spoke, I watched my mother's face for her reaction. I wanted to know if she knew what she did, and if so, if she felt remorse.

She looked like she was learning the news for the first time. She was shocked, horrified, and upset. She seemed deeply ashamed of what she had done, of what she had allowed to happen. I don't have a word to describe her expression, a mixture of sadness and shame. Whatever it was, it was enough to make me feel sorry for her and stop talking about it. I felt bad that she had to live with knowing what happened. I learned from her lack of explanations and apologies that she couldn't be held responsible for anything that happened in my life. It's strange to me now that I felt bad for *her*, but this was the beginning of me feeling sorry for my mother.

I felt sorry for her, instead of feeling sorry for myself. Even then, I think I was still uncomfortable with feeling sorrow for what had happened to me because we are generally uncomfortable when people feel sorry for themselves. We've been told to pull ourselves up by the bootstraps, keep our chins up, not be a baby, not be weak, not dwell on the negatives. Since then though I've wondered whether thinking that way is helpful. I don't want to feel sorry for myself, but sometimes I don't know how else to feel. I am more and more convinced that knowing how to feel sorry for ourselves is actually the beginning of understanding compassion and what it means to feel sorry for others in a good way.

God would eventually rescue me from the hopelessness I learned as a child in that apartment. He also would soften my default reactions of fear and mistrust in relationships. But it would take a long time to recover from the loss of trust and the feeling that no one was looking out for me. My dark and hopeless days were not over yet.

4

THE SADDEST SEVEN-YEAR-OLD
ON A PLANE

When I was seven, I went to visit my father for the summer in Florida. I hadn't seen him at all in four years. Four years without a father isn't good at any age, but to a girl who hasn't seen her father since she was three, it is a lifetime of sadness and longing. The first couple of years without him, I cried and asked my mother for him repeatedly. Then one day I stopped asking for him.

I'm not sure what prompted my father's reentry into my life, but suddenly it was June and I was seven and on my way to see him. It was my first time on a plane, and I was alone with only the flight attendant to guide me. I wasn't scared or worried, though, and since I was the only child on the plane, I felt like I'd been given a pass into grown-up world for the day.

The summer seemed to last forever, until all at once it was over. That's how it feels when you're a kid. Time stands still, until the earth is broken under your feet. And so it was for me—the summer ended, and it was time to go back to California to my mother. Only I wasn't ready to leave my father again. My older brother and sister lived there too, but it was my father I was afraid I'd never see again. Those four years without him had left their mark on me.

When it was time to go, my father took me to the airport and walked me down the corridor. The flight attendant was waiting for me at the gate. I refused to go and held onto my father's leg, crying and saying no. I remember his eyes; he was crying too. I don't remember what he said, if he said anything. I don't know how he finally got me on the plane. I think I finally went limp and followed the lady down the jetway.

On the plane, the flight attendant showed me to my window seat near the front. I was still crying. I sat down and pressed my cheek against the cold window. I can still see my face, looking out the window of the plane as I cried and cried and cried. My eyes were red, and my tears were hot. I'm sure I looked like the saddest seven-year-old on a plane anyone had ever seen.

I looked out over the clouds and sky that separated me from the man I needed the most. The thought that I might never see him again was the only thought in my head. I was inconsolable; only exhaustion finally relieved me. I must have fallen asleep, since I don't remember waking up or getting off the plane. It almost felt like a bad dream. I floated through the hallways back to my mother and returned to my life without him. I saw him again the next summer and every summer after that, but it didn't matter. I never recovered from losing him that first summer.

I later found out I wasn't the only one who never forgot the seven-year-old getting on a plane crying. After I got married, my father began to get sentimental in our conversations. He often mentioned the time he took me to the airport and I wouldn't let him go. He got the age wrong; he kept saying I was three. Then I realized he was talking about when my mother left him and took me to California with her.

All those years growing up without him, I assumed he didn't think about me. I thought he didn't want me, or worse, didn't love me. I didn't hear from him for four years, so what else was I to think? I know a lot more of the story now, but as a child, when entire portions of your life are missing, you assume the worst. It's taken me decades to believe anything different. I still talk to my father. The conversation has changed, but the man is still the same.

I've often wondered how my life might have been if my father had been around when I was a young girl. Would I have looked for so much attention elsewhere? Would I have found it easier to believe God was really there and actually cared I was alive?

Little girls need their fathers. The fact that my father was not around helped cement one of the most formidable, complex set of lies of my life:

> You may have a father, but you can't be with him. He's too busy. He's not interested in you. He can't be bothered with you. You aren't good enough to be interesting. You aren't beautiful enough to be noticed. You aren't performing well enough to be approved of. You simply don't matter that much. Fathers have better things to do. God has better things to do too. He has a whole universe to run, after all. He let all this happen to you; can't you see you don't matter to him?

Forty years later, I am still fighting to believe the truth instead of those lies. Without a loving father's consistent presence, the ultimate lie that God is not good is much easier to swallow.

5

THE BIG CATHOLIC FAMILY AND WISHFUL PARENTING

I'm not really sure how this came about, but in the summer of 1981, when I was eleven years old, my mother sent me to live with a large, Catholic family. I can only assume that my mother left me there because she went traveling with Richard and it wouldn't have been romantic to have me along. I asked my mother, but she doesn't remember.

I didn't mind living there; in fact, I thought it was pretty great. I felt like part of their family. I don't remember any of the kids' or parents' names, but I remember moments. They had a fairly small house for such a large family. I think it was a trailer. I don't remember much about that time, other than that I didn't feel lonely there.

Some of my favorite times were sitting around the table for dinner. They gave me rosary beads, and I held them during prayer and sneaked peeks whenever everyone else was praying. Some of the kids giggled and peeked too. I liked it, even though I didn't understand what they were doing.

I don't think they had much money. One clue was that they drank powdered skim milk. I don't know why anyone would drink that unless it was to save money. It didn't seem like an option not to drink it, so I drank it too, while holding my nose.

Everyone, including me, had chores to do, and—I'm not kidding—I even *liked* doing chores. Doing chores with everyone made me feel useful, like I had a purpose. It passed the time during the day and made play time that much more fun. Chores are a good thing in my opinion.

I loved that summer. I mostly didn't even miss my mother, except for one time when I was in the hospital after I was in a golf cart that flipped over. My face and eyes swelled up so much that my mother didn't even recognize me when she first saw me. Fortunately, I recovered quickly, and the rest of the summer returned to a nice blend of chores, play time, and family meals. It felt so normal. My whole life as a child and teenager consisted of wanting to be "normal." Yet my life was anything but.

I enjoyed the adventurous nature of that summer and remember it as the one time I honestly wouldn't change a thing (except maybe the golf cart accident). I loved that family, and I loved who I was with them. I became a risk-taker and a people-watcher. I miss that about my eleven-year-old self. I found my first surrogate family of many I would have in my lifetime. I lost a summer with my mother, but I gained a new family, if only for a short while. I also gained a lifelong love for substitute-family dinners, rituals with deeper meanings, chores, long summer nights, and lying outside under the stars. It turned out to be one of the best summers of my life.

I share this story for a couple of reasons. One is to make clear that my early years were not all bad and that even then my life was a mixture of good and bad times, light and dark times. I also share it because I think it demonstrates what I think my mother was hoping would always be true when she left me with other caretakers: that I would have a wonderful time. While thankfully the summer with the Catholic family was a wonderful experience, that clearly was not always the case when she left me with someone.

I don't believe my mother intentionally set out to hurt me in any way. I just don't think she thought about how her choices would affect me. In general, she seemed to just be trying to survive and hope for the best in any situation. I have since come to call my mother's general parenting style Parental Wishful Thinking. I would not recommend it. Sadly, it is all too common.

Wishful Thinking Belief #1

Living in a small town will take half the work out of parenting. You can let your kids run around outside and around town unsupervised, and they'll be safe. Small towns are full of wonderful, God-fearing, simple people. It's more likely that child molesters live in big cities. So your kids are probably fine. Send them to church to give them something to do and a way to make friends. Don't worry about going with them; they don't care what you believe anyway. They'll be fine as long as you keep them busy. When they grow up and wonder why you never went to church, you can tell them you didn't really believe in it for yourself but you wanted them to go because it was good for them.

Wishful Thinking Belief #2

Teach your daughters that their appearance is what makes them worthy. Make sure to only emphasize how pretty they look, how nice their hair is, how tan their skin is, how wonderful it is to be tall, how lovely they look in dresses, how pretty their smiles are, and how nice their outfits are. Make this the most regular message you speak to them. Also, when noticing other girls, make sure to only remark about their appearance as well. And don't forget to regularly remark about your own weight, wrinkles, height, skin, hair, nose, hands, legs, and feet. Be consistent in your message: Women are valuable if they are beautiful.

Wishful Thinking Belief #3

Don't talk about physical affection (kissing, hugging, hand-holding) or being affectionate, and definitely do not talk about sex or anything else marriage-related. There will be time for that at some point in the future. Whatever age your children are now is too young. Don't worry about them talking about those things among themselves; they probably will *never* do that. Being in an uncomfortable, awkward conversation is worse than death itself, so at all costs avoid making yourself or your child feel weird. Since your parents never talked to you about sex and most people you know don't talk with their kids about it, your kids will probably be fine.

So, sadly, from my mother I learned that I'm not safe or protected in this world and need to look out for myself. I learned that I would be left and that no one would come for me until it was too late. I learned that my value lies in my physical beauty. I also learned that sex is simply unmentionable—so dangerous, mysterious, inappropriate, private, and complicated that it should not be discussed. Sex of any kind, before marriage or even in marriage, is too scandalous to be talked about, ever. It would be many years before I unlearned those lessons and learned hopeful lessons grounded in truth instead.

LOST

6

SENT AWAY ON A ONE-WAY TICKET

The summer of 1983 I was thirteen and had been living for a year with my mother and her boyfriend Robert. She started dating Robert after she divorced her second husband, Richard. My mother and I had moved to a condo in a different part of San Diego, but I don't remember actually moving. It's not surprising that I don't remember since I paid little attention to anything my mother did, and we certainly never talked through anything together. It was the summer after my first year of junior high and the end of my year-long reign as an out-of-control teenager, although I didn't know it was the end yet.

I was on my regular flight to Florida to see my father for my annual summer visit. I'd been flying there every summer since I was seven. The summers were the only time I saw my father during the year. When my parents divorced, they had no formal visitation arrangement, which is part of the reason that I didn't see my father for four years after they divorced. Four years is a lifetime when you're a kid. But I was thirteen now and everything was about to change, again.

This summer was supposed to be my routine visit. However, I

was in for a big surprise once I got there. I had no idea beforehand that I was being sent to live with my father permanently. After I'd been there a few weeks, my father started asking me repeatedly if I'd like to live with them. That wasn't even an option in my mind. "Uh, thanks, but *no*," I said. But he kept asking. Then one day he said, "Well, you're going to live with me for a while." No explanation, no reason. "Your mother and I have decided," I was informed.

I was reacquainted with powerlessness. It was a new year, a new town, new "caregivers," and I had no control again. I had no say in the matter and no voice, even about my feelings. I was too young to leave, get a job, or have any money of my own; I had no choice but to stay. The feelings that accompanied helplessness felt eerily familiar.

I was in shock at first, then devastated. I remember standing in the hallway when he told me. A random conversation in the hallway while he walked to the kitchen. I felt like time stopped, and I was in an alternate universe. This could not be happening, I thought. I remember looking down the hallway to my room, and it was like one of those movie scenes where everything becomes exaggerated and the edges are cloudy. The hallway seemed longer than usual. The narrowness of the hall got even smaller, and the beige walls seemed translucent. I felt like a ghost. For a moment, I was five years old again and trapped. It was happening again. I died another mini-death that day.

I never saw my room back in California again—all my things, my posters, my bed, my clothes, my stereo, my books, my photo albums . . . all gone. I don't even know what my mother did with them. She probably packed them up in boxes, intending to return them to me at some point, but never did. My whole life was in that room. When you're a teenager, your room is the place your personality is expressed and your dreams take form. And all at once, it was gone, just like that.

My stepmother didn't seem to like me much, or at least that's what I thought. She was put in an awkward situation herself and had trouble hiding her unhappiness about it. Who could blame her? She had a toddler of her own to raise, had just finished ten years with my sister, and was about to only have two years left with my brother. Then another one of her husband's children comes to live with them. I'm sure my father merely informed her too—no notice or choice on her part. Unfortunately, knowing she wasn't pleased made it that much harder for me to adjust.

I hid in my room a lot. Not having to share a room was a gift. My older sister had recently graduated from high school and would leave for college at the end of the summer. My brother and I got along, but he was a junior year in high school and had a girlfriend, so hanging out with his younger sister wasn't a high priority on his list. The only other sibling in the house was my half-sister, and she was three years old. We were an odd bunch of kids in that house.

I was angry with my mother for sending me there without telling me. I can't remember exactly how long I didn't speak to her, but it was a long time. I wrote her letters occasionally, but that was it. When I turned sixteen, I called her and told her I understood why she did it. I didn't like the way she did it, but I understood why.

I was a wild teenager when I lived with her. I was overly interested in boys and stayed out at my friend's houses all the time, way too late. I didn't listen to my mother or respect her. I didn't do what she asked of me. I would even sneak out of the house at night to be with my friends. I had tried drinking and smoking pot by age thirteen. It sounds incredibly young, but it was California and it was not unusual at that age—literally everyone was doing it. Even my next-door neighbor's parents smoked pot and let their kids do it with them. It wasn't legal then, but it was no different than cigarettes to most of the people I knew.

My mother didn't know what to do with me. She was a mild-mannered person and definitely not a disciplinarian. Her boyfriend lived with us, which I did not like. He was nice enough, but he was eccentric and much younger than my mother. The whole situation was uncomfortable. She worked all day and spent the evenings with him. She did what she wanted, and so I thought I could too. There was a lot about the situation that wasn't stable or healthy. Like most teenagers, all I cared about was having fun. I didn't care about school. I wasn't involved in athletics anymore. I didn't go to church anymore. I just had friends. I always had friends.

Only in hindsight can I say my mother probably did the best thing for me at the time, but I hated being lied to. I felt like she tricked me, because she had to, to get me on the plane. I didn't exactly straighten up when I moved to my father's. It took three more years before that would happen. In fact, I grew more wild and rebelled against every restriction put on me for a while. If I had stayed in California, I likely would have ended up pregnant. I don't think I would have become addicted to drugs because they were never a big temptation for me. I wasn't interested in any other drugs besides pot and I was scared to try anything more serious. I didn't really like drinking either. I guess I wasn't wired to be an alcoholic or a drug addict. Unfortunately, that didn't mean I wouldn't struggle greatly with other more socially acceptable addictions, like food.

But even after I came to some acceptance of my mother's decision, I have never understood how she could give me up. I also probably never understood the desperation she must have felt in order to do that. Regardless, to say the transition to living with my father wasn't easy is an understatement. After I got there, I spent the greater part of three years pushing back against my parents, life, and anyone that tried to control me.

Not surprisingly, that was the year I began to become overweight. Prior to that, I was a healthy weight and size by anyone's standards. I was never more than five pounds overweight, if that. After I moved to my father's, I was more anxious and insecure than ever. I would hide in my room and bring boxes of crackers and cookies with me and sit on the bed, calming myself with food. I overate at dinner—a stressful time because my father and stepmother were always tense or bickering. I overate after dinner because cleaning up was my chore, so I cleaned the plates with more than the sponge. I started gaining weight slowly, about a pound a month, ten pounds a year. By the time I was eighteen, I had gained fifty pounds. I couldn't pretend anymore that everything was alright; my body was telling on me.

If I could change one thing about that time period, I would have been told the truth about what was about to happen when I got on that plane. I know I wouldn't have liked it, and I would have had a fit, but I wouldn't have been lied to. Most of my teenage years were an uneasy mix of rebellion, performing for approval, and sadness. I didn't enjoy high school. I was too serious about everything and always anxious at home.

Ultimately, my mother's hopes for me came true. I turned into an obedient child and successful student, eventually. The path to get there was not pretty. And even though I was obedient and successful, I wasn't healthy, and I didn't feel loved. I grew up and forgave my mother for sending me there without my knowledge. But I have never adopted the idea that it is sometimes okay to lie. Also, speaking from a teenager's point of view, I think I should have been allowed to take some of my things, or have them sent to me. It might have made the adjustment to my father's house a little easier, and maybe it would have made his house feel more like home.

7

ACTING OUT . . . AND OUT
AND OUT

Trying to control another person, especially a teenager, through guilt and manipulation usually backfires. My parents found this out firsthand.

My mother sent me to my father, in secret, to try to get control of me. My father put me in private Christian school to try to get control of me. My stepmother verbally abused and shamed me to try to get control of me. The school principal and teachers enforced overly strict rules to try to get control of me. Unfortunately for all of them and for me, life for the next three years would be an exercise in futility and a disaster in the making.

Looking back, I always wondered why no one asked me *why* I was acting out so much. No one took the time to sit down with me, look me in the eyes, ask questions, and listen. I know it can be excruciating trying to talk to teenagers. I didn't make it easy. But isn't it the job of the parent to at least try? It all goes back to relationship—in particular, the fact that I didn't have a strong one with any of my parents or caregivers. I certainly didn't trust my parents, and they didn't trust me. I looked and acted like a "fast girl," or as my stepmother liked to call me, "a slut." I already believed that about myself, but something about someone who didn't care about me calling me that made me angry.

So there I was, thirteen, trapped in my father's house, living with my stepmother who seemed to hate me, my brother who was too old for me to hang out with, and my half-sister who was too young. So I sought solace wherever I could find it, usually in the company of my friends and boyfriends. The title "boyfriend" sounds more serious than it was because we didn't do anything but hang out and kiss. I didn't care about doing anything else; I just wanted to kiss whoever I thought was cute. It was fun and made me feel good. I went over to a friend's house whenever I could. I had so many sleepovers and dinners with one friend's family that they should have charged me rent.

In the summers, I went to camp at Florida Bible College in Orlando, where my older sister went to college. There were always plenty of cute boys there. My sister's roommate even had a brother who was cute and interested in me. We started dating, which sounds innocent enough until you hear that he was twenty-one and I was only fifteen. Now it's creepy and inappropriate, or at least it should have been to anyone paying attention. But no one was. So I did what I wanted, no matter how stupid. Fortunately for me, the guy never tried anything with me. This was a good thing, since the following summer we were still dating, and I lived at my father's hotel in Miami Beach, totally unsupervised.

My father had separated from my stepmother that summer and moved me with him for a while to a hotel he owned on South Beach. It was an old 1950s-style hotel right on the beach. This was before the art deco district exploded and South Beach became all the rage.

This living environment was less than ideal. My father worked all the time, and having that kind of freedom at fifteen, with all the hormones, was a total disaster. I took it upon myself to do whatever

I wanted. There was no shortage of bad decisions that summer. I was still in the midst of my three-year rebellion, and acting out was my modus operandi. I was out of control, and no one even noticed.

That fall, at the beginning of my sophomore year in high school, my father and I moved back in with my stepmom and little sister. My plan for a life of unobstructed fun was still in place. My father, though, surprised me by telling me I would be switching schools and begin attending Dade Christian Academy, another private school closer to home and away from my friends and bad influences. My brother had graduated and left home, so it was just me and my little sister there now.

At that point in life, as far as anyone was concerned, I was a "bad girl." I'm not proud of this title; in fact I was ashamed of it for a very long time. My parents also found out I was having sex in the most embarrassing way. My brother took it upon himself to tell on me when he found out I wasn't at my friend's house, but at my boyfriend's house. I found this hypocritical, since my brother was sleeping with his girlfriend at the time, but I guess I was younger and a girl, so he saw that as enough cause for sibling betrayal. The reason it was so embarrassing, though, was because my brother didn't tell me he had told my father, which gave my father the opportunity to catch me in a lie. He asked me the next day how my sleepover was at my friend's house, knowing full well where I'd actually been. When I said it was fine, he yelled at me: "You're lying to me and that's the worst thing you could ever do!" The feeling of being caught in a lie is the worst kind of unpleasantness for a teenager. The jig was up.

I was punished harshly for my behavior, and I'm not just talking about no TV or allowance for a few months. I was put on restriction for an entire year. I could only see one friend, the daughter of my father's work partner. I couldn't go anywhere but to school and sports practice. I couldn't go out with anyone but the one girlfriend for the entire year. I was trapped. I couldn't believe this was happening to me. I didn't have a car yet, and even if I did, I wouldn't have had anywhere to go. My rebellious streak was involuntarily over.

8

BEING A GOOD GIRL

The next three years, my last three in high school, were the Good Girl Years. I didn't surrender to my father's rule; I resigned. Since I was fully grounded my entire sophomore year, I had a lot of time on my hands and started studying more and doing better in school. I went on my first church mission trip. I got involved in youth group. I started dressing modestly because I wanted to. I only had one boyfriend, and he was a decent guy, thankfully very respectful. We only hung out at each other's houses when our parents were there, and we never did anything but hold hands and occasionally kiss. This was a whole different world for me.

I excelled in school and sports, namely volleyball and softball. I played basketball, but was terrible at it. I signed up for it so I wouldn't have to go home after school and be alone with my stepmother. My father was always working until late in the evening, sometimes 8 or 9 at night. But even with basketball, good things happened. I was part of a team, and those were my main friends. I was good at volleyball and softball, so when those were in season, I felt valuable. My softball career didn't end on a high note. The last game of my senior year, I was up to bat with two outs, the bases loaded, and I hit a ball straight to the left fielder. That was it, the game was over, and I would never have a chance to play another game in high school again. It was a depressing moment. I cried and left the field alone. What a bummer of a way to end my high school softball experience.

Things were still tense at home. I never felt comfortable there. My father was always working, and my stepmother always seemed upset about me existing. I didn't watch much TV and there was no internet in the '80s. I spent most of my time in my room listening to music and doing homework.

Music was a lifesaver for me. My love for music started in the '70s. Even though I was only ten or eleven, my brother was listening to Boston, Led Zeppelin, Rush, Aerosmith, Van Halen, and Eric Clapton. My mother introduced me to James Taylor, Carly Simon, The Eagles, and Jackson Browne. This was the music of my childhood and still some of my favorite listening today.

So one evening, I was home alone with my stepmother. She had been drinking, although I didn't know it at the time—she hid her wine well. I assumed she was in a bad mood. She started yelling at me, telling me how horrible my real mother was. I don't know what set her off, maybe being stuck in that house with me while my father was off working. I don't know what she was hoping to accomplish by yelling at me about my mother since I didn't choose my mother or choose to live there. I think my stepmother just needed to vent, to make someone else feel as bad as she did.

She followed me around the kitchen, down the hall, and even into the laundry room, yelling at me the whole time. I didn't yell back; I was trying to get away from her. I finally went back to my room, shut and locked the door, and turned up the stereo loud. She began banging on the door and yelling. Eventually I couldn't take it anymore and decided I had to get out of the house. I admit that my thought process was not thorough since I had no car, and it was after 8 p.m. I was a responsible runaway, though, because I remembered to grab my uniform since we had a softball game the next day. I grabbed all my books for school, along with some clothes and shoes, and I ran out of the house. She followed me out the door yelling, but stayed in the foyer as I ran down the street.

I went to the neighbor's house two doors down and asked if I could use their phone. I have no idea what they must have thought when a crying teenager showed up on their doorstep, but they let me in, and I called a friend. She and her mother came and got me. I went to their house, and they set me up in the spare room. Finally, I was safe. I would end up living with them for a few weeks. I told my father I wasn't coming home. He didn't even argue with me about it. He actually even put me up in a hotel for a few nights. At the time I thought it was cool; now I think it was ridiculous and inappropriate. He didn't know what to do with me or his wife. She was probably yelling at him and making life miserable for him at home, and I was sixteen and refusing to come home—not a good situation for anyone. I eventually did return home, and of course we never talked about the incident. Everyone acted like nothing had happened, and daily life went back to "normal."

I never wondered about it then, but many years later I would look back on that time and wonder what the adults were thinking in these scenarios. I knew what my father wanted: for me to be good and stay out of the way. I knew what my stepmother wanted: for me to disappear. I knew what I wanted: control over my life. But that was something I wouldn't have for a long time. Being a good girl was another attempt at gaining control. My father gave me the idea that if I was good enough, everything else would fall into place. When I returned home from my suburban runaway experience, he gave me a talking to on the porch before we went in the house. He said, "You just be so good that she can't say anything about you— you just be perfect, dammit!" So I tried to be perfect, I tried so hard.

My junior year, I brought home all As and only one B on my report card. I was happy and excited to show my father. I'd never done that well before and was certain he would be pleased. He took one look at the report card, looked at me seriously through the top of his glasses and said, "What's happening with this B here?" I was crushed. I always fell just short of his approval.

So apparently being good wasn't all it was cracked up to be. I would have to find a new strategy. The trouble was, I had tried everything. So I kept to the course and did my time at my father's house until I graduated and could leave for college. Acceptance and approval would have to be found elsewhere.

During this time, I never sensed that God was looking out for me, and I certainly wasn't looking for God, even when I started going to church activities and on my first mission trip. I just wanted away from my family and to spend time with my friends. But God was looking for me. I ended up meeting some of the coolest people I have ever known while at that church. My motives were all wrong, but God wasn't deterred or offended. He was with me all along. I just couldn't see it yet.

9

BREAKING FREE

August 1988, the end of the summer after I graduated high school, my father's house in Miami was about to see the last of me for the next three years. I had no intention of ever going back, although I did eventually; even a rebel's resolve wanes over time. I packed up my candy-apple-red Pontiac Firebird with all my clothes, music, and pictures and headed to Palm Beach Atlantic College. I was so ready to start my new life as a free woman. The reality was that I was not a woman, but a child. As quickly as I embraced my freedom and newfound place in the world, I got lost again, and for a long time. While I was free from my parents, I became a slave to my appetites and all the world had to offer me.

The first year and a half of college was like an extension of high school, but with less accountability and more access to boys and pot. For the first time in my life, no one was asking me where I'd been, who I'd been with, or what I'd been doing. This kind of freedom alone was exhilarating. Even though it was a private, Christian college and there were some rules, like a curfew for when to be back in the dorm, the contrast to life at home was staggering.

There was electricity in the air—anything was possible. Unfortunately, the most interesting possibilities for me involved college romances and hanging out with friends. I went to class, but learning was low on my list of priorities. I liked the environment of college; I had little interest or focus in attaining an education that would serve me later in life.

For most people, college is a place where you begin forming your identity apart from your parents and high school friends. You start asking questions like: Who am I now that I don't have to worry about parental approval? What will I do with my free time now that no one is expecting me to be home at a certain time? What do I really believe about being a Christian, going to church, and serving God? What do I want to do with my life?

I lived in the only on-campus house; the rest of the dorms were typical apartment-style buildings. Our house was more like what you would see in the movie *Animal House*. There were fourteen girls in that house, with two bathrooms—two—and they were very, very small. We all had a fifteen-minute limit in the bathroom each morning. I still don't know how we survived or accomplished getting ready each day.

One very good thing that happened that year was that I met my best friend, Lee Ann. We're still close friends today—more than thirty years later. Lee Ann was my Resident Assistant, and she had the best room in the house, along with her own bathroom, which I coveted.

That year I also had an economics professor, Dr. Wharton, who became friends with Lee Ann and me. We would go over to his house and hang out with this wife and kids. We babysat his daughter occasionally. I remember several things about him that have stayed with me all these years. He was a student advisor, so I went to see him a few times in his office. One time he said, "Whatever you do, don't get into debt." Unfortunately, I recalled that more *after* I got into debt, wishing I had listened to him.

I also remember his interactions with his son when he was

misbehaving. Dr. Wharton didn't yell or scream or throw a fit. He simply changed the tone of his voice and calmly but firmly said his son's name. His son clearly understood his father meant business. I was always impressed by that. All Dr. Wharton had to do was change the tone of his voice and his son knew he was serious.

Dr. Wharton always listened to anything we had to say. He seemed genuinely interested and amused without being condescending. We had dinner at his house, and he often read from the little book *Our Daily Bread* before saying prayers and having dinner. It made me feel like dinner together was about more than just eating. His family and this time in college were gifts from God to me. I was reminded that loving families do exist, time around the table is time well spent, and people can change the world one person at a time. He changed mine.

10

WANDERING

I wish I could say I stayed in college and listened to all Dr. Wharton's sage advice. Instead, in what began a series of bad choices, I dropped out of college the second semester of my sophomore year. I had no direction, no vision, and no family support. I became solely focused on making money to sustain my partying lifestyle. This quickly became the driving force of my life.

My first real job was as a receptionist at a prestigious law firm in West Palm Beach. The firm was in a high-rise black glass building known as "The Darth Vader Building." It overlooked Palm Beach Island and was pretty impressive to a young professional wannabe like myself. The firm had more than thirty lawyers and ninety employees total. Every day felt like I was starring in an episode of the '80s TV show *LA Law*.

I was making three hundred dollars a week answering phones, smiling, and looking pretty at the front desk. I couldn't believe people got paid that much for doing so little. I told myself I could always go back to school and study during the day at a job like this. Of course, I never studied at work, even when I did go back to school. I was more interested in reading magazines (the '90s equivalent of surfing the internet). Five years later and only a couple of classes closer to finishing my degree, I realized how much of a trap making money could be. For a young college student with no accountability or goals, money was the shiniest prize of all.

It wasn't a total waste of time—more like a detour. As I became bored with receptionist duties, I learned how to be a secretary and eventually became the secretary to the comptroller. In addition to a wide range of administrative skills, I became comfortable working with professionals in a variety of disciplines: lawyers, clerks of court, paralegals, legal secretaries, and clients. I felt confident in an office environment, and professionals didn't intimidate me. I developed an identity of my own as a young professional administrative secretary. It was easy to do in a firm like that, surrounded by lawyers and suits while getting paid more than some of my friends who had college degrees. Meanwhile, my original plan of completing my degree slipped further away. Like most things in life, I didn't notice it while it was happening. I woke up one day twenty-five years old, in debt, living paycheck to paycheck, no real relationships—only fleeting romances, and no vision for a better life. For all intents and purposes, I was floundering.

During my fifth year at the firm, the administrative assistant resigned, and I decided to make a bid for the position. My hopes were quickly dashed after talking with my boss, who explained to me it "wasn't going to work" because I was too young and would be in charge of women much older than me, which wouldn't go over well. I was disappointed. This was the only opportunity for advancement in the firm. So I had a choice to make. I could stay and do the same work for another ten to fifteen years and reapply for the position, or I could look for something else. I chose the latter.

A friend of mine had recently left the firm and started working for a real estate company. She quickly became a property manager at one of their residential leasing complexes and was making excellent money. She convinced me to try working for her. I resigned from the firm a few weeks later and began working as a leasing agent at one of the apartment complexes. It was a relatively easy gig: show people apartment models, fill out applications, take deposits, smile, look pretty, try to sell them on the property. I did okay and made a little more money than the law firm, but I was still directionless and couldn't see a future there.

My friend John was living in Tallahassee, and I drove up regularly on the weekends to see him and hang out with his girlfriend and other friends. It was a fun college town, and we always had a great time. One day we were talking on the phone, and as I bemoaned my situation John stopped me and said, "You need to just move up here and finish college at FSU. Work and finish school—there are plenty of jobs here." I'm not sure whether it was his assertiveness and confidence that it was the right decision for me, or if I was desperate for a change, but I did it. I gave my two weeks' notice at work, notified my landlord and roommate, sold all my furniture, and within three weeks moved from West Palm Beach to Tallahassee.

I made a few trips to interview for jobs and was able to obtain a position as a legal secretary at a prestigious law firm. However, when I arrived in Tallahassee, they informed me that they had chosen to eliminate the position. I was rattled. I'd just moved across the state, given up my job and apartment, only to have no job upon my arrival. I hustled and got busy working as a temp. Thankfully, one of the firms hired me full-time, and I was only out of a job for about two weeks.

That job lasted two years as I worked during the day and went to classes at FSU at night. Unfortunately—and all too common—the man I worked for was verbally abusive and physically inappropriate. I was caught off guard at first and didn't quit working there right away. I kept showing up to work, trying to pretend everything was fine. But one day I was short with one of our clients on the phone, and it surprised me. I realized I was unusually irritable and tense. I knew something had to change. I started looking for other work then, and when I got my first offer I gave my two weeks' notice.

The next firm I worked for was a small litigation firm run by a father and his two sons. I learned how to become a legal secretary there and would go on to stay with them for the next ten years, until I got married and moved out of state. Both brothers were easy to work for—polite, respectful, and easygoing. I couldn't have asked for better bosses. I continued to take classes at FSU at night and worked my way through college, eventually graduating at age thirty-one. My bachelor's degree was in sociology and economics because I was originally interested in development in Majority World countries. But when I graduated, the only jobs in that area were in research, and the salary would have involved a significant pay cut. Additionally, the lawyer I was working for gave me a substantial raise, making it even more difficult for me to leave for a low-paying research job. So I stayed at the firm for another six years after graduation.

For the most part, I liked working for lawyers. With few exceptions, I found most of the lawyers I interacted with to be respectful, intelligent, and decent people. But I eventually became bored and frustrated, more with life than with work. Every day was a grind, and I felt trapped—a slave to my bills and mounting debt. I could have tried a different career, but I wasn't motivated enough to go back to school at thirty-six to earn a master's degree that may or may not result in a more interesting career. Fortunately, when I got married the following year, my husband's career allowed me to try something new. Since I didn't have to worry about obtaining a certain level of income, I could simply do something I was passionate about. So for the next seven years, I worked for nonprofit organizations, championing various causes from education to international aid. It was a welcome change of pace.

In high school, I envied my fellow students who seemed to know exactly who they wanted to be and what profession they wanted to enter: doctors, lawyers, veterinarians, accountants, missionaries, teachers. But I had never felt confident about the direction I should go. I didn't feel passionate about anything, and if I did, my fears dissuaded me from trying. My difficult childhood, not surprisingly, led me to an interest in psychology. So my senior year of high school in Florida, I decided I wanted to move back to California, study psychology, and attend Biola University.

For the first time, I felt excited about a potential career path. But I never made it to California, even though I applied and was accepted to the program. I became crippled with fear about moving 3,000 miles away from anything and everyone I knew—an example of being comfortable in known misery rather than exploring the unknown. People like to say they have no regrets because their choices made them the person they are, but I don't mind saying I have regrets. I regret not following that dream. I'm not sure I would have become a psychologist or therapist, but I would have enjoyed learning about a subject I was passionate about. I chose a safe path instead. I studied business at a college ninety miles from home.

As far as the world and my parents were concerned, I was a success. The truth was that even though I managed to graduate college, I had no real skills. Learning information is not the same as acquiring skills. I also had no idea who I was in the world or how I would change it for the better. I simply had a degree and some life experience. I don't regret finishing college. I simply wish I would have followed my instincts and chosen a different path through college. Instead, I earned a bachelor's degree in economics, trying to make my father proud and trying to look important. I worked at law firms and other professional jobs trying to earn the most money. I worked at nonprofits trying to "make a difference" and be useful. All the while, I was bored in class and at work.

I discovered that making your parents proud isn't more important than doing something that makes you come alive—which ideally also would make them proud. After paying bills, I spent most of my income on frivolous things, like sushi and new shoes. Even the nonprofit world proved disappointing. Sadly, corruption and power struggles exist in that field as much as any other. There's a certain kind of moral fiber and stick-to-itiveness required to get past the corruption to do the good work. I didn't have it then, mostly because I didn't have the emotional health to stay focused on the greater importance of the work. I was exhausted from trying to find my significance in work and be useful all the time. I would be forty-five before I realized that if you're not grounded in something larger than yourself, it's easy to give up and feel hopeless about changing yourself, much less the world. I now know that success is a lot more about who you are rather than what you do. Fortunately, it's never too late to change and grow into a more honest and grounded person.

11

BEING SINGLE: THE LONG AND WINDING ROAD

There's a great line from the TV show *Sex and the City,* where Charlotte says, "I've been dating since I was fifteen. I'm exhausted, where is he?!"[1] I can relate to this. I started dating at fifteen and didn't marry until I was thirty-seven. After twenty-two years, I was exhausted.

I was hooked after my first kiss and first boyfriend. It was sixth grade and neither of us knew how to kiss, but I had been practicing on my hand (like you do). He was tall and lanky and tan, with perfect teeth, brown eyes, and brown hair. He would become my physical archetype. On our first date, we went to see the movie *Raiders of the Lost Ark.* Our moms dropped us off at the movie theater, which was at the mall. I remember he had his arm around me for most of the movie, but about halfway through he said, "Liz, I really like you, but my arm hurts, so I'm going to move it, but I really like you." He was a nice boy. I remember when we broke up. I was at his house, in his room, sitting on his twin bed. I don't remember much of what he said. After my tiny little sixth grade heart realized he was breaking up with me, the rest became a blur. I remember being devastated and crying giant crocodile tears, as if someone had told me my dog had died. He was calm and matter of fact about it. He wasn't mean or frustrated, though he did seem confused as to why I was that upset. He was right to be confused—I took the relationship way too seriously. He was cute and nice though. The rest of my dating life would be downhill from there for a long time.

While it might be mildly entertaining, I'm not going to chronicle those twenty-two years of dating. Most of the stories are either too embarrassing for words or simply sad tales of naiveté, willfulness, and desperation. I went about dating in all the wrong ways until I was well into my thirties. I was definitely looking for love in all the wrong places.

There seem to be specific phases of dating that people go through. From ages thirteen to eighteen, dating consisted primarily of hanging out or making out, not exactly relationships. Through my college years, I continued this type of hanging out and hooking up more than anything else. From twenty-two to twenty-five, as a young professional, some actual dates occurred (outside a living room or couch area). By the time I reached twenty-five, there was some weekend travel and more outings, including dinners, movies, and parties.

I was in two serious relationships during this period: one when I was twenty-five and one when I was twenty-seven, each lasting for about nine months. I thought I was ready for marriage but wasn't and really shouldn't have even been dating. After the latter breakup, the next two years were by far the loneliest of my life. Many women dread turning the big 3-0, but twenty-nine was much worse for me. At twenty-nine, my most recent boyfriend had moved on and gotten engaged within a year of our breakup, leaving me to feel like the oldest single person on earth. I can laugh now, since I just turned forty-eight, but at the time I felt so old. That was the beginning of what I call the Extreme Isolation Years: twenty-nine to thirty-three. Not surprisingly, those years gave way to the somewhat-absurd-but-interesting Internet Dating Years: thirty-three to thirty-six.

Fast-forward to the end of the dating scene for me when I met my husband through eHarmony. Back in 2006, using online dating services was still somewhat taboo, but mostly embarrassing. The unspoken view was that you must be desperate if you had to go online to find someone. I thought that too at first, but I tried for years to meet someone at church or through friends, and nothing was working.

Then one day one of the guys in our church singles group shared how he had been secretly dating a girl for six months who he met online. He didn't want to tell us right away, in case it didn't go well. But it was going great, and they ended up getting engaged, so he was excited to share his happy news. He certainly didn't fit the description of a desperate single person. He was a lawyer, confident, good-looking, and intelligent. This was the beginning of my perception change about online dating. Don't get me wrong, I still didn't want to meet someone using the internet, but I felt I had to at least be open to it.

It took me three years to find my husband once I started using eHarmony. I met fourteen different men in person and was matched with countless others before finally meeting the man who is now my husband. The stories of these meetings are full of the ridiculous and the mundane. Let's just say that I paid my dues. My husband, on the other hand, only met one other woman before meeting me. So unfair. I still wince a bit when telling the story of how we met. My husband, however, loves to tell the story.

Maybe it's possible to have a fun, exciting, and relatively pain-free dating life. I wouldn't know and have never met anyone who has, but that doesn't mean it doesn't exist. Even if you have a great upbringing, wonderful self-esteem, healthy confidence, and solid boundaries, dating remains an awkward and often painful experience for most people. American culture seems to increasingly run on instant gratification, chemistry, and individualism, and nowhere do we see this more than in dating culture. This was certainly my experience. I've never been happier than when, at the age of thirty-seven, I waved goodbye to those twenty-two years of dating. Being single was hard. Being married is also hard—but I'm thankful to have a companion I trust to share life's joys and sorrows. To anyone currently dating, I hope you have faithful friends. I hope you live your life knowing you are truly loved. That's what matters in the end. The rest just makes for an interesting read.

SEEING THROUGH THE DARKNESS

12

BLOOD: THICKER THAN WATER

W hat's the first word that comes to mind when you hear the word "family"? I like hearing people say things like "love," "home," or "joy." I truly do. Even though I can't choose those words myself, I never begrudge anyone a happy childhood or a loving family. For me, though, the first word that comes to mind is . . . "complicated." So family is a tough subject for me to write about. While I wish parts of the stories were different, my family has shaped much of who I am. To leave them out of my story would be like leaving out the salt and sugar from a recipe—the result would be bland.

We aren't a family with a lot of so-called "Hallmark moments." We aren't a particularly close family, emotionally or geographically. Now that we're all adults, we are spread over several states, including North Carolina, Georgia, Colorado, and Florida. Many of us aren't in touch anymore except for a few times a year. Some of us don't talk at all. Historically, we haven't been an open or communicative family. Like a lot of families, we have a lot of hurt and secrets.

All families are dysfunctional at some level, all the way back to the first family that ever existed. So the fact that mine is dysfunctional is not unusual. Every family is unique and personal. When we share our family stories, we see common threads.

My family members are full of stories—so many, in fact, that each one of them could write their own book. This is only my story. Their stories belong to them. I have no intention or right to tell their stories unless they've given me permission. As you read, know I'm only sharing what I've been given permission to share.

When I decided to write this very personal book about the things I've observed and learned in my life, I wasn't sure how I would talk about my family. When I think about each individual member, I can recall some happy memories, some favorite personal characteristics, and even some good stories of influence and inspiration. But in many ways my family has been a great source of pain for most of my life. I still love and care for them, but I love them in a nontraditional, unsentimental way, because it's the only way I can. Whenever I try to act traditionally, in a way that seems expected of me, I'm always frustrated or disappointed. So years ago I began trying to find a new, more honest way of being with my family. It's far from perfect and there's plenty of room for growth, but it's a start and is definitely more peaceful.

By and large, my family doesn't tend to bring out the best in each other. There may be love between us, but it's hard to get to. Consequently, we don't live most of our lives together, and the fact that we share the same bloodline makes us a family more than anything else does.

The saying "blood is thicker than water" originally meant the bond between comrades in war is stronger than family allegiances. The water portion of the saying can be traced back to a proverb: "The blood of the covenant is thicker than the water of the womb." Which means we've actually got it backwards: the "water of the womb," or our family relationships, are not as strong as the "blood of the covenant." Rather than "blood" shared by family, the original interpretation of the term was literal blood. In other words, the blood shed by soldiers on the battlefield makes for stronger bonds than bonds of the family you were born into. This makes much more sense to me, especially considering my particular family. Many of my friends seem more like sisters or brothers and fathers or mothers to me. I will always feel something special for my actual blood relatives, but it doesn't feel stronger—it just feels different.

I was in college before I began thinking about my family relationships on a deeper level. I was curious and confused at the same time. For reasons still unknown to me, my father and mother told me little about their families, my extended family, so I know almost none of my family history. My aunts, uncles, cousins, grandpas, and grandmas are mysteries to me. In addition to not living near them or visiting much, I don't know them well at all. Both sets of grandparents have passed away. For all intents and purposes, we are all unknown to each other and connected only by blood.

As children, we didn't spend much time with extended family either, except the occasional holiday or random visit. Whenever we did visit, I always enjoyed being around both my aunts and cousins. They were funny and smart and seemed to like me. I can't say I really knew who they were. I would have liked to have known them, but it almost feels too late or too hard to know them now. Maybe they feel as I often do, that seeing immediate family close by is all they have time for. Maybe they have other reasons for not staying in touch. I don't know. My aunt on my mother's side lives in Florida with her husband and is not interested in a relationship with me. My aunt on my father's side is close to her son, and they are both close with my sister, but apart from the occasional card or phone call, we aren't close.

As a child, I only saw my uncles once or twice, and again as an adult only a few times. One of my uncles has since passed away; the other uncle is still living, but has never kept in touch. None of my extended family, with the exception of my aunt on my father's side, came to my wedding or graduation from college—events even families who aren't close usually attend.

Being part of a family means you learn your place and what role you play. In my immediate biological family, when I wasn't absorbed with survival and pleasure-seeking, I functioned as the peacemaker, although not in the traditional sense. I made peace through humor, distraction, or changing the subject. I was the funny, happy, cheerful family member. I was definitely a conflict avoider. I observed everyone. I tried to calculate their next moves. I was always trying to read the situation or the mood of whoever was in the room.

I learned it was a bad idea to disagree with others. So I rarely, if ever, disagreed with anyone in my family. If I did, I was shamed and faced hostility, primarily from my father, but also from my brothers. I learned early not to disagree with anyone, or I would be the recipient of anger—whether outright, passive-aggressive, avoidance, or being cut off altogether.

I also learned it wasn't a good move to express sadness in conversation. I rarely saw my mother cry, although she looked sad most of the time. It was mostly a sadness veiled by attempts at putting on a happy face. I saw my sister and brother cry at various times, but we never talked about it. I would only cry when I was alone, if I could help it. My father became angry if you cried. I remember one time I was upset and went to him crying. We were in the kitchen, and he slammed his fist on the counter and said, "Stop crying, I cannot handle hysterical women!" There was nothing hysterical about it; I was just crying and talking. But I learned never to come to him like that again.

In our family, if you had an opinion, you weren't taken seriously—at least I wasn't, perhaps because I played the role of the funny one. I could only be seen in one-dimensional terms: silly, funny little sister or daughter. My brothers and sisters had their own roles. My older brother was the dominant one, my sister was the humble one, and my other brother was the smart one.

In families we learn what's expected of us. Even though I was the youngest, I was expected to help my siblings however I could.

That was my duty as their sibling. If I didn't help or couldn't help, I was shamed and looked at as disloyal and selfish. My parents had the same expectations for my duty toward them. Even after I moved out of the house, went to college, and got a job, I was expected to help them in whatever way they needed. Most of the requests didn't come until I was a young adult, working.

My mother often seemed content to play the victim of unfortunate circumstances. She would ask for help with her finances and budget. She never seemed able to save money. My father was more subtle. He also had problems with finances and overextending himself in debt. He would ask for help, but he made it seem like he was helping me by paying me back with far more than he borrowed. I learned early on that it's not usually a good idea to mix finances with family, but I didn't break away from many of these unhealthy family patterns until I was in my early 30s. When I did, I was initially seen as selfish, disloyal, uncaring, spoiled, and even sinful—mostly by my father, but also by my brother Michael.

The underlying messages my family unintentionally taught me were that I was only loved when I was giving other people what they wanted, that I was only important if I put their needs before my own, that I was only worthy when I was pleasing people, and that my sole purpose in life is to make other people happy. These messages left me lost. I would have to unlearn them before the way ever became clear.

13

FATHER: POWER

My father had a lot of power over me growing up, first during the years I grew up without him and later when I tried and failed to keep his attention. Through him, I learned that you don't have to be present to have power over someone. Sometimes a person's absence is the most powerful mark they leave.

At 6'3" and 220 pounds, my father had an intimidating presence. He had thick dark brown hair, broad shoulders, and glasses and often wore tennis shorts with Cuban shirts and loafers without socks. His ankles crackled when he walked, especially in the morning. He fell asleep watching TV at night, and if you walked in the room and woke him up he would always say he wasn't sleeping, just resting his eyes. He was a strong physical presence—you knew when he was in the room.

I try to remember that my father was once a baby, child, teenager, college student, single man, and husband, all before he was my father. It helps me see him as a whole person, not only who he is to me. For most of my life, there was only the man I knew as my father—someone there and not there all at the same time. He was a complex figure with a big presence and mysterious heart.

I still don't really know him, but as he nears eighty-one years old and struggles with failing health, I am beginning to see a softer side. I'm grateful to see it, but sad for the pain he's had to endure for it to surface. I would have liked to have known this softer person growing up. Maybe things could have been different for me, for all of us.

Born in the winter of 1938 near the end of the Great Depression, my father was the son of a Jewish mother and Methodist father. He was raised Jewish and converted to Christianity as an adult, around age thirty-three. He grew up in fascinating times. He lived under Presidents Roosevelt, Truman, Eisenhower, and Kennedy. He was only three when Pearl Harbor was bombed and only seven when the atomic bomb dropped on Hiroshima. During his youth, rock n' roll entered mainstream music, NASA was formed, and the Peace Corps was created. He was not in the military, but married and started a family during the Vietnam War. He was around to see Martin Luther King Jr. come on the scene and be assassinated. He witnessed the country in shock when JFK also was assassinated. He witnessed The Beatles arrival in America and Neil Armstrong's landing on the moon. These were monumental times, though like most people, he probably didn't realize it at the time. I never heard about any of these events from my father; I read about them in books.

My mother said my father wasn't around much when I was young. She said he was always gone working at the financial services company he owned. She said he wasn't there for any of our births either. My mother even birthed me at home without him or anyone else present to help, because she couldn't get to the hospital in time. My older brother, then seven years old, helped her call the hospital to talk her through the delivery. I have no memory of my father until I was seven, but I felt his absence during that whole time.

My father is a complicated man. He's intelligent, witty, stubborn, and intense. He's always been extremely occupied with religious study, specifically Christianity. He's also ambitious and driven and has always been consumed with his work. At home, he was often irritable, tired, and distracted. For many years, my experience with him was limited to trying to get and keep his attention. He could also be demanding, controlling, and verbally explosive. I wasn't worried about being physically struck, but I feared upsetting him. His voice was enough to keep me on guard. I simply wanted him to love me and be proud of me, like any kid.

I learned a lot from my father, including some things I don't think he intended to teach me. I learned that the only way to get his attention was to look good, perform well in school, be funny, and if all else failed, get in trouble. Otherwise, there was simply no time or need for me. I was born into an unhappy marriage, the fourth and final child. My parents divorced when I was three. My mother sent me back to him when I was thirteen. To my father, I was a problem to be handled. I needed to do a few things and a few things only: go to church, read the Bible, stay out of my stepmother's way, not cause problems, not do drugs, and not get pregnant. This was my high calling.

After I grew up and left home, whenever I would call to talk to him, my father reaffirmed these were still the most important things to him. Often he would answer the phone and say, "Everything alright? You're not pregnant, are you?" No Dad, I'm calling to say hi. To which he would commence the standard questions about my grades, my weight, and my church attendance.

Later, after I got married, he was softer and told me regularly how proud he was of me. I'm not ungrateful, but it felt a little late. I needed to know he loved me and was proud of me when I was a child. I learned how to grow up and live without his approval and acceptance. When he finally told me, I didn't need to hear it anymore.

He's changed the last few years—some humility has surfaced. I am thankful I get to see it. He struggles now with a heart condition and has endured several strokes and heart attacks. His body has shut down and recovered multiple times. I'm not sure how much longer he has to live. I've prayed for his suffering to end and for him to have peace. That's all I can do. We've talked several times over the last few months, and each time he's said I love you and I've said I love him too. And I do. I wish we could have had more of a relationship. I wish I had known as a child that I was loved.

My father gave me what he could, what he thought was enough, what he was taught was enough. It was my father's approval, not my mother's, I've always craved. And not merely his approval—I wanted his adoration. I also wanted to be like him. I wanted to be powerful. I did become like him in some ways. I can be overly critical, manipulative, and impossible to please. I haven't been able to completely change these things about myself no matter how hard I've tried. It reminds me of the great power all fathers have. We hear little kids say all the time, "Do you see me, Dad? Dad, look!" A content smile comes over their faces when their father turns their way. That's what I wanted, to be seen and loved.

14

MOTHER: REMNANT

I read the definition of "remnant" recently and thought of my mother. *Remnant: a small, remaining quantity of something.*[1] A quantity or quality of something remained about her. My mother didn't have an easy life, growing up or later as an adult. As a child, she had an alcoholic father who beat her and her mother regularly, so her mother left and raised my mother without him. She was raised in part by her grandmother and even lived in foster homes for periods of time. My mother's sister only recently informed me that she and my mother had been abused by family members, repeatedly, in the most horrific ways, when they were children. I never knew any of this about my mother when I was growing up. I was in my forties before I knew any real details about her upbringing. When I would ask about it, she said she couldn't remember much from that time of her life. Now I understand why.

It has become important for me to remember that my mother, like my father, was not always only my parent. Before I existed, she was a child too. It's especially helpful for me to remember her childhood when thinking about how I was raised. It's amazing she survived her childhood at all, much less became a mother herself.

She suffered a thousand tiny deaths during those years, yet she managed to live. Her spirit grew quiet, but a remnant of her remained.

I know that she was born in Atlanta, Georgia, graduated from high school, worked at a bank, and went to a business college but never graduated because she got married instead. Before marrying my father, she dated another man, but they broke up after high school when he joined the military. I often wonder what her life would have been like if she had married that man instead of my father. No doubt she's wondered that many times herself. She met my father at age nineteen. He was a dance instructor. She married him when she was twenty-one and had her first child at twenty-four, then another, then another, then me. Her choices weren't unusual at the time; after all, that's what most people did. It wasn't uncommon to meet and marry young, start a family, and have one child after another. It's still a common path.

When I grew up and got married and began to think more deeply about my life, I still wanted to ask her many questions. So I decided to write her a letter. It was a hard letter to write, even harder for her to read, I'm sure. We've been to counseling together and made peace with each other over many issues. I have her permission to share the letter I wrote. My hope is that my honest questions might help someone else. For many, the mother-child relationship holds more questions than answers, and most of those questions never get asked.

This letter was written with the intent to heal myself and maybe even my mother, if she let it. I was done blaming my parents for the way my life turned out. I was instead seeking understanding. I had serious questions and felt I had the right to ask them. I didn't have high expectations in terms of answers. The power to ask, in many ways, was enough for me. Here is my letter:

Dear Mom,
    I've always wondered what you were thinking when . . .

You chose to divorce my father.

You chose to move 3,000 miles away from him, making it very difficult for him to see me.

You chose to leave your two children with him.

You chose not to see those children more than a handful of times over twenty years.

You chose to marry another man who didn't have any interest in your children.

You chose to travel with this man and regularly left me with people who were not family and who I barely knew. Where did you go and why didn't you take me with you?

I have excused or justified your behavior my whole life, telling myself the same things you told me: "you did the best you could."

But if you can't be held responsible for your actions, who can?

I know my father is also responsible. This is not about blame for either of you, it is about understanding. I want to understand.

This is not about forgiveness. I have forgiven you as you have forgiven me for many things. This is about the consequences of those choices for both of us.

I have lived a large part of my life anxious, lonely, insecure, repressed, and quite sad. I tried to hide all these feelings and focus on being happy. I think you lived this way too. This makes me sad for both of us.

As long as I can remember, I learned how to distract myself from any real feelings and stay absorbed in other things: television, movies, food, boys, school achievements, sports, and hanging out with anyone who was around. I did anything I could to escape. Did you do this too? Is this how you survived?

I spent most of my life looking for love and acceptance from men. Why didn't you ever talk to me about sex? I needed to know the truth. Why didn't you tell me how much it would hurt me physically, mentally, emotionally, and spiritually? I know you didn't want to think about it. I understand now you weren't taught either.

Still, why didn't you ask me yourself or someone else what could be going on with me at thirteen, that I would be acting so reckless and seeking so much attention? It's not common to be that wild that young. It wasn't just hormones. I understand you didn't know how and it was uncomfortable. I know it would be hard for me, even at my age now. But isn't that the price and the privilege of being a parent?

For all these reasons and more, I never wanted to have children. For the entirety of my twenties I was sure of it. I wasn't sure I would have had the parenting skills to do any better than you did. Your mom didn't teach you, and so it goes. I don't remember you teaching me anything about art or drawing or painting or creating. I don't remember talking to you about anything—friends, school, life lessons, right and wrong. You sent me to other people to do that: church, school, live-in nanny, other families. I know now this was your experience too. Consequently, I have mastered the art of other things: worrying about how I looked more than the kind of person I was, remaining disconnected from family, creatively disabled, trying to escape the slightest conflict or problem at all costs, and the worst skill of all—not feeling my life. That all changes now. I am changing it.

Thank you for being willing to let me ask these tough questions. I know it was hard. Life is changing again. I'm getting older. You're older now too, you remind me of it often, as your body grows tired and your last years are upon you. My wish for you is that you would know it's not too late. It's not too late to feel your life, in all its sorrows and joys. It's not too late to forgive and be forgiven. It's not too late to write and sing and do all the things you've told me you always wanted to do. I hope my last years are filled with purpose and with a surplus of friends, wine, flowers, coffee, and books. I want you to have all of this too.

I love you, Mom. I do.

The truth is my mother is a wonderful person, with many gifts and endearing qualities. She passed down traits and preferences I treasure: her sense of style (classic and elegant with a touch of artsy); her love of good, healthy, whole foods; her gentle way of speaking and listening to people. She is never forceful or pushy. She is not rude or impolite. She is a gentle person, something the world could use a little more of.

One of the hardest things in life is trying to understand how some of the most wonderful people can do (or allow) some of the most terrible things. It's one of life's great paradoxes. When I hear the painful stories of other people in different situations, I sometimes think: *Oh, I would never do that.* But I do other things—things that hurt people, things that leave a mark. I do them for all kinds of reasons. And who will be the judge of me? Until I understand and accept that I am capable of the same horrible things, I will never have compassion for my mother or anyone else.

My mother's legacy will be her children and the children she's cared for over the course of her career as a nanny. We all must decide what kind of marks we will leave on the world. I don't know what my legacy will be. I've chosen not to have children of my own. I still made my mark here, though. I'd like to think I will live on in some way in the hearts and minds of the people I loved: my friends and their children, my stepchildren, and my siblings. I have loved them, and love lives on when everything else fades. As little love as my mother received as a child, the miracle is she found a way, if only at times, to give what she did not have. I found that way too. And for that I am grateful.

15

BROTHERS: SHADOWS

My brothers are important to me, even though we have very separate lives. We've lived apart most of our days, only living in the same house as children a few years at a time here and there. They're both older than me: Bryan seven years older and Michael four years older. I have loved both of them equally, though differently. The reality is they are more like shadows to me—passing in and out of my life, full of mystery and darkness.

Bryan

Bryan was the oldest of the kids and the one who moved with my mother and me to a small town near San Diego after our parents divorced. Bryan was ten when we moved there, and I was three. I vaguely remember following him around, trying to get him to play with me, but I don't really have any other memories of us growing up together. I know both of us had dogs, played outside, and had upstairs bedrooms across from each other. We shared the house with my mother and Richard, my stepfather, for a few years before

Bryan went back to live with my father in Florida. That's really all I remember.

I only saw Bryan a handful of times over the next twenty years. He moved around a lot. He didn't go to college. He had a lot of girlfriends. When I was nineteen, he began writing me letters for a short period. They were handwritten and talked about what kind of trouble he was in, his girlfriend at the time, God, and spiritual things. He told me he loved me and would visit me when he could. I liked getting his letters even though they sometimes made me sad.

He did come see me for a while but was soon on the road again. He met his wife a year later. I'm not sure how long they dated, but it was brief. His wife's family threw them an extravagant, country club wedding. It was funny to me seeing my brother all cleaned up in a tux. I'd only ever seen him with a bunch of tattoos and in board shorts, headed out to catch a wave at the beach. He seemed happy, so I was happy for him. They have been married for twenty-eight years now and have one daughter.

Bryan and I always got along and had fun when we were around each other. We just didn't have a lot of years together. As adults, I was in his wedding, and he came to mine. We've seen each other when visiting our parents. I wish we were closer, but that's not the way our family works. I never stop wishing all good things for his life. In our family, that seems to be the best we can do.

Michael

I haven't spoken to my brother Michael in more than five years. When I saw him five years ago, it had been ten years since I had seen or talked to him. It's not because I don't love him—it's because I can't live with a broken heart. My brother has been struggling with drug addiction and bipolar disorder for the last thirty years. He has been unable to stay clean for more than a year at a time. That, coupled with his bipolar disorder, has left him with an extremely difficult life, barely surviving while trying to outsmart his addiction. He struggles every day to stay clean and manage his mental illness, yet he cannot seem to get well. I don't understand it, and I cannot help him. I've tried, and it almost killed me.

Michael and I became close in high school and early college, before he was diagnosed with bipolar disorder and before he began using hard drugs. Michael had joined the Air Force after his first year in college. This is where he was diagnosed with bipolar disorder and honorably discharged. The years following his discharge were filled with a series of jobs, including one as a broker at Prudential where he started abusing cocaine. He eventually became addicted. I spent the next several years visiting him in rehabs, halfway houses, and even jail.

By the time I was in my early twenties, Michael had been arrested several times for various things: driving without a license, driving on a suspended license, drug possession. The only time he went to jail was when he got stopped for speeding in a small town and was found to be driving on a suspended license again. The judge gave Michael nine months in jail, one month for every time he got a ticket for driving on a suspended license. Michael couldn't get out of it this time. I went to see him regularly at the small jail. It broke my heart each time I had to leave and see him walk away behind the bars again.

It became unbearable for me to watch him suffering so much. I couldn't help him, although I tried every way I could think of. After five years of being closely involved as he spiraled out of control, I finally had to walk away. I was anxious and worried about him all the time. I began having nightmares of him dying alone in a hotel room from a drug overdose. These dreams were so real, I would wake up with my heart pounding, sweating, and having a hard time catching my breath. I knew I couldn't go on like that. So I made the decision to distance myself from him, my brother whom I loved. It was one of the hardest things I've ever had to do.

Even though I have nothing but compassion for him now, for years I was angry with him. He hurt me, and not just me, but himself and everyone in our family. He couldn't seem to stop. He did the things most drug addicts do: he lied, stole from me, yelled and cursed at me, told me I was no better than him. And he was right; I'm not. I am simply making different choices. I don't know what kind of choices I would make if I had his challenges. But as a twenty-something, all I could see was that he was hurting everyone, including himself, and it made me angry. I couldn't understand, and he didn't make it any easier for me because of his hostility when I tried to talk to him. It was hard to feel compassion for him when he was yelling and cursing at me for not helping him. This was what drugs did to him. It turned him from a fun-loving brother into a manipulative bully who was angry if you didn't give him what he wanted. It broke my heart. It still does.

I'm not going to pretend I understand addiction—its causes, cures, or otherwise. The only thing I know is what it's like to be the sister of an addict. As hard as it has been, I know now it is harder to be the addict. I didn't believe this until the last ten years or so, and sometimes I still get angry. But mostly I try to imagine what it would be like to have your mind and body constantly trying to destroy you, day in and day out, all day long, with no relief.

While I've never been addicted to drugs, alcohol, or cigarettes, I certainly have more socially acceptable things that I orient my days around and feel I can't live without. My addictions don't cause me to be ostracized from society. They don't limit the type of job I can get or whether or not my relatives will agree to see me. My addictions are more "soft-core." They are things I reach for to comfort me, distract me, dull me, soothe me, and give me happiness. I reach for food, television, movies, books, work, and companionship. Before I was married, I reached for men, as many as I could. Like my brother always said, I'm no better than him. He was right; I'm not.

So where is the grace in my brother's life? I think it's been there all along. I think he's been given a lot of opportunities, love, and support from family, even if misguided or incomplete. It never seemed to be enough. My brother's illness seems to steal everything from him. My father and sister try to help him and be involved in his life. I don't know whether it has helped. I just knew that I couldn't be involved and also go on with any quality of life. I tried to listen from a distance for a while and assure him of my love, but listening wasn't enough.

When I realized I wasn't helping either of us, I began to do things differently. I have my own choices to make and I have to keep making them. I need healthy boundaries and have to decide how much I will expose myself to unhealthy patterns. I have to protect my family and my property. I have to decide when and how much to communicate with him. I can't do much, but I can do these things. I can ask for help. I can pray. I can never stop loving him. But he cannot define what love is. Addiction defines love as the unconditional giving into demands. The word unconditional threw me at first since that's how I wanted to love him. If you know and love an addict, you know this cycle all too well.

I miss my brother, the one I think might still be inside the person he has become. I miss the guy who used to brush my bangs to the side, laugh with me in the car on the way to school, go to dinner with me in college, and listen to good jazz when we were older. We went to comedy clubs and open mic nights and talked about life. He used to tell me the birthday cards I gave him were just like me—funny on the outside and serious on the inside. That was my brother; he knew me, and we understood each other. But that was a long time ago. Even though he's still alive, I feel like I've lost him to drug addiction and mental illness. I miss him. I want my brother back.

16

SISTERS: SECRETS

I have two sisters. My oldest sister, Jen, is my biological sister and five years older than me. My other sister, Melissa, is my half-sister and a little more than ten years younger than me. I don't remember much about growing up with Jen since I was only three when we all lived together. After the divorce, as with my father and other brother, I wouldn't see her again for four years. My two sisters and I share more than biology—we share secrets. Not the harmless kind you tell after lights out at bedtime; the kind that have the potential to destroy families. The secrets my sisters have are theirs alone to tell. But because my sisters' lives are intertwined with mine, I obtained their permission to share a portion of their stories here.

Jen

I started flying back and forth from California to Florida in the summers beginning in 1977. I shared a room with my sister Jen when I was there. My brothers shared a room down the hall. I only remember splices of summers with my father, like going to church on Wednesday nights and out for ice cream afterwards. I'm sure we went to the beach and the mall and maybe even played in the neighborhood, but I don't remember any of that.

We went to a Baptist church. My father seemed to know the important people there. I was baptized at this church after I became a Christian. I was seven years old. I still don't know if I understood what becoming a Christian meant. My older sister Jen simply asked me if I wanted Jesus to come live in my heart and told me he died for my sins. It sounded like a good thing to me, so I said yes and was baptized several weeks later. Jen was happy for me. I was happy too, for a while.

I saw Jen every summer for the next six years. When I was thirteen and came to live with my father permanently, Jen had recently graduated from high school and was leaving for college. So I moved into her room and she moved into the dorms at Florida Bible College. I saw her randomly over the next five years for holidays and semester breaks and such.

After Jen went to college and began working, I didn't hear much from her until she was in her mid-twenties. I only saw her occasionally over the years, so we grew apart. I didn't know what was going on with her until she was about twenty-six years old. The next five years of her life were heartbreaking and difficult. She went through a series of unspeakable traumas. The secrets she carried were all coming out—she hadn't willingly told them, but her body and mind began to break down under their weight. That was the year I went to see Jen in the hospital, where she told me she had been the victim of a violent, sexual assault. I've never seen her so scared and so broken. Watching her suffer through this horror, and the subsequent mental illness, changed the way I looked at the world. It also changed the way I thought about God. The God I had constructed made sense until then. I had to question everything now.

My sister is a kind and loving person. Growing up, she was gentle, dutiful, and quiet. She never bothered anyone. She loved to play the piano and sing. She didn't date much in high school, she wasn't a social butterfly, and she was never in trouble. She had friends, went to school, sang, and played her music. She would go on to college and eventually graduate with a degree in music education. She wasn't into drugs or drinking or parties. She kept to herself and her circle of friends. Why would God allow the most horrible things to happen to a person like her?

There are no satisfying answers for these questions. Yet I continue to ask. The deepest question we have, if we believe in God at all, is: Are you good? How then do we reconcile his goodness with the horrible injustices in our lives and the lives of others?

My sister has to live with PTSD now for the rest of her life. She has to take a lot of medication to function and get through each day. She works a full-time job serving people with mental illness. She has her own apartment, car, and pets. She has good, loyal friends. She visits family once or twice a year. She goes to church and work and to her friend's house. She is still kind to everyone, even those who have hurt her. She does not complain. She works hard. She cares about her family. She takes responsibility for herself. She does not drink or use drugs and hasn't for more than twenty years. She wakes up every day and chooses to live.

My sister accepts the things that have happened to her. Not me. I still have trouble accepting them. It makes me angry and it makes me sad. And maybe that's okay; because sometimes being angry for someone is a sign you're still alive. I want to do something about it so other people don't have to go through what she did. So I will look for ways to do that. I will try to be aware and look for those ignored or taken advantage of. I will ask questions, and I will listen.

Melissa

My younger sister, Melissa, was born three years before I moved to my father's house. We didn't spend a lot of time together, mostly because she was so young and I was a teenager. We passed in the hallways and looked at each other across the dinner table. When I started driving, she rode with me to school, but again, because of the age gap, we didn't talk much. Occasionally when she was very young, she would try to antagonize me, like toddlers do. One time she went into my room and stole my lipstick. When I caught her, she ran down the hall and began writing on the wall with it, rendering it a mushed, broken mess. It wasn't a big deal, but I still remember the mischievous look on her face. She was taunting me and it worked. It's one of the few funny stories between us now. We didn't keep in touch much for more than twenty years. But in the last ten years we've become good friends—something more important to me than family.

Melissa and I did have one particularly significant bonding moment during her childhood. Unfortunately it was brought on by our parents' fighting. I was sixteen and she was six. My father and stepmother were in a particularly heated argument. You could hear them at the other end of the house. They came out of the bedroom, and my father was at one end of the hall and my stepmother at the other. They were screaming at each other. At one point, my stepmother threw a vase that hit him in the head. He was bleeding and looked like he was about to explode. Melissa was crying. I quickly picked her up, carried her on my hip outside, and tried to comfort her. She hugged me until she felt better. Eventually, things inside the house calmed down and we went back inside. I assumed it was an isolated incident in our childhood. I was wrong. Recently she told me this violent behavior continued when she was left alone with my parents after all of us moved away. Now, when I think of packing up for college, I wish I could have put that scared girl in the car with me. I wish we could have broken free together.

FINDING MY WAY

17

FRIENDS: MIRRORS, WINDOWS, AND DOORS

Some of the best moments in my life have occurred in the company of true friends. Some of my worst moments also have been held safe and healed through their presence.

Maybe you, like me, have friends who are as important to you as your family, or are more like your chosen family. Maybe these types of friends are more like extended soulmates, filling our souls in unique ways. The kindness friends show isn't sentimental stories —these friends change your life and your character. They can inspire, challenge, and soften the blows life gives. Friends come and go in our lives, much like seasons. The friends who have impacted me the most, for better or worse, have been like mirrors, windows, and doors. They reflect my true self back to me, let the light in, and sometimes open the way to a new path I might not have chosen. All of these friends have been in my life for a reason—to change me, to wake me up, to toughen me, to heal me, and to love me. They are my favorite gifts from God and the primary reason I believe he is real.

At times I have needed my friends too much. I looked to them for things they weren't meant to solely provide. I didn't understand at the time why I was doing it, but I understand better now. I was looking for them to provide some of the things healthy families usually provide: support, encouragement, security, identity, and love. Growing up in a household like mine, friends become more than just people you hang out with—they become lifelines.

No family is perfectly healthy, but I have known a few that hit close to the mark. Many of these people became second families to me, something lost kids like me really need. God provided these friends not because I deserved it, but because he loved me. Even friends who hurt me ended up leading me toward a better path than the one I was on.

Mirrors

The most genuine and loving friend is the one who reflects back your true self. This isn't always pleasant, but that depends more on you than the friend. The friend most like a mirror shows you your best and worst, but always tells the truth. They see you as you are. They reveal what others see, even if you may have trouble seeing it yourself. The kindest friend will highlight the best in you and let you decide how to deal with the worst. These friends can say hard things, things you may not want to hear but know are true, and encourage you to be better. Delivery is everything in this area; the skill of speaking the truth in love needs cultivating.

When I was in college, I made my first real best friend. Lee Ann was joyful and full of life. She taught me how to have fun without drinking or getting into trouble. She introduced me to sushi and step aerobics and how to artfully display a breakfast plate. More importantly, she taught me how to be authentic before it became a cliche.

Whenever we'd talk about religion or faith, Lee Ann would always say in her funniest Southern accent, "If it ain't real, it ain't right." That statement has stuck with me through three decades of navigating suspicion when religious people claim things about God. Those words helped me as I was growing my own faith. Every time I was tempted to posture, I'd think of her words. Be real.

Lee Ann has remained a lifelong friend. I have a few other friends like this, but not many. I don't think people can handle more than three or four mirrors at a time. Lee Ann and I share almost everything, from deep belly laughter to dysfunctional family secrets. But what we share most is a real, sometimes painful, mostly joyful, genuine faith. This is the kind of friendship that lasts; this is the kind you pray for.

Windows

A less common friend-type is the one that reminds me of windows. They can be understated or grand, and come in all shapes and sizes. But one thing they all do is let the light in. I need light in my life, lots and lots of light. Sunshine makes me come alive, heals my soul, and inspires my mind. I also appreciate soft light—lamplight instead of overheads, dimly lit cafes, and candlelight. The light I'm speaking of here is the light of truth. Lies are covered in darkness; light shines and can bring the truth—sometimes gently, sometimes brightly.

I have a wise and gentle friend named Kim who has been like a beautiful window to my soul. I was in my late twenties when I met her and her husband. I had been looking for genuine Christians to live in community with. The first thing I noticed about them was their eyes seemed filled with light. I had only seen that once before at the church in Key Biscayne. Genuine spiritual life and truth is surrounded by light. Windows also let fresh air in when opened, and like a breath of fresh air, a truth-telling friend can awaken your soul.

My friend Kim has this kind of effect. It makes you want to be around her as much as possible. So that's what I did. I was single and had a lot of time on my hands in the evenings. They were married with four young children and needed more time than they had. This seemed like the perfect opportunity to help them get a much-needed date night once a week. I began going to their house every Thursday to sit with their kids while they slipped away for a few hours. I loved seeing their faces change from the time they left to the time they returned home. I helped them, but they really helped me. I got to be in their charming home, with their adorable kids, doing simple things, and experiencing the joy of self-forgetfulness. For a few hours every week, I stepped out of my little world and into theirs. I'm not sure who looked forward to Thursdays more, me or them. Kim is a steady, calm presence and has been a faithful friend of mine for almost twenty years. This quote from Thomas Merton always reminds me of Kim and her husband Mike:

> I just remember their kindness and goodness to me, their peacefulness and utter simplicity. They inspired real reverence, they were saints in that most effective and telling way: sanctified by leading ordinary lives in a supernatural manner, sanctified by obscurity, usual skills, common tasks, routine. But skills, tasks and routine which received a supernatural form from grace within.[1]

Doors

The next kind of friend might seem less desirable at first glance, but they are actually what we need in certain seasons. They are like doors. No matter what kind of house you live in or path you're on, doors are needed to get where you're going. I'm referring to those friends who were once very close but after certain events, conflict, or time, have parted ways, and it's left a mark. I've had a few of these friends, and I'm sure I've been one of these friends for some. During the height of these friendships, you can't imagine ever being without these friends. During the lows, you can't flee fast or far enough. When a friend cuts you, intentionally or not, the wound is deep.

We are drawn to certain people as friends for a variety of reasons. Sometimes we connect with people because of things we have in common. This may be harmless enough, but if the things you have in common are ego-related (pride, selfish ambition, or insecurity) they can become unhealthy ties. It's not always easy to recognize these connections. People can be intelligent, clever, and interesting, while at the same time lacking in the character qualities that make for a good friend, like being humble, kind, and trustworthy. What can start off as a seemingly fun friendship can turn into something else. The important thing is to realize when it's time to part ways. In my opinion, that time is when neither of you are making each other a better person, or when the majority of the time, one of you feels drained with every interaction.

This is where I think of friends as doors. Doors in and of themselves are neutral. They can open the way to a cozy, comforting space; they can slam in your face; they can usher you onto a new, more desired path. It takes strength to walk through these doors. It takes courage to start a new friendship or leave an old one. It takes wisdom to know when to stay and when to leave. No friend is all good or all bad. We would all do well to accept each other's rough edges and be more gracious. That's not what I'm talking about here. I'm talking about knowing when a season of a friendship is over. We don't like to think about friendships ending, but in order to be healthy, some of them must. Friends are friends forever is a nice saying, but it's not the whole picture. I have some friends I hope will be friends forever. For the others, I'm thankful they were in my life at one time, and I'm thankful to be on another path now. Even the best friendships have limitations. Henri Nouwen describes this well in his book *Life of the Beloved*:

We need friends. Friends guide us, care for us, confront us in love, and console us in times of pain. God gives us the friends we need, when we need them. But friends cannot replace God. They have limitations and weaknesses like we have. Their love is never faultless, never complete. But in their limitations, they can be signposts on our journey towards the unlimited and unconditional love of God.[2]

18

SIGNIFICANT OTHERS: NOT EVERYONE YOU LOVE YOU MARRY

I didn't get married until I was thirty-seven, and I started dating at fifteen—that's twenty-two years of dating. More than two decades of being intrigued, confused, angry, happy, distracted, disgusted, delighted, and close to despair about ever meeting someone I could call husband. Not everyone I met along the way became significant, but a few had a lasting impact and changed me for the better. I'd like to honor them and myself by naming some of those I loved. There are people you love who become a part of you, whether you marry them or not. I think that's a good thing. It's not a betrayal of your future spouse; it's a sign you were willing to love. Even though pain and loss occurred, goodness remains.

The number of people I dated over those years is too high to count. The number of those who loved me is exactly five. I didn't marry them, but I would have. I wonder sometimes what life would be like if I had. I don't regret not marrying them; in fact, I'm grateful I didn't. I think it's important to name who you loved or who loved you, even if you choose to marry someone else. I chose my husband. I love my husband. I can't imagine life without him. I also loved each of these men in different ways and am better off for having known them. God used each of them to show me different facets of love. Some names have been changed to protect privacy.

Stephen: Respect

I met Stephen when I was just fifteen. I'll admit, I had no idea what real love was, but looking back, he was the first man to treat me with respect while simultaneously adoring me. He wanted to get married as soon as I graduated from high school. I was less sure. Being the somewhat rational person I was even at fifteen, I said, "I love you and all, but I want to go to college first and not be married while I go." This was the first of a few wise decisions I would make concerning men. Stephen and I had a sweet, young love, marked with lots of laughter, chemistry, genuine kindness, and care for each other's well-being. He loved me and I loved him, as much as we knew about love at the time. He wasn't going to be my husband and I was certainly not going to be his eighteen-year-old wife. I'm thankful I knew him. He showed me that it's possible to have chemistry with someone and not act on it. He was the first of a very few men who would prove this was true.

Phillip: Honor

I met Phillip when I was eighteen and in my freshman year of college. I was in full party-girl-mode the first semester and mainly interested in all the wrong kinds of boys (wild and charming). Phillip was quiet and sweet. He wasn't wild and didn't talk a lot, so he was easy to miss if you weren't paying attention, which I wasn't. I knew he was interested, but I was occupied with other boys. I can't go back, but if I could tell my eighteen-year-old self anything, it would be: *Look for the quiet ones, the honorable ones, the kind ones. Stay away from the wild ones, the charming ones, the flashy ones. You'll be glad you did.* Of course my eighteen-year-old self wouldn't have listened because I had to learn the hard way.

Phillip and I stayed friends over the next four years. I became friends with his sisters and would regularly hang out at his house. His dad was a pastor, and I started going to his church. I loved being around his family. They weren't like any Christians I'd ever known. They also liked being around each other. Seeing a family who enjoyed each other fascinated me.

One day when I was about twenty-three, Phillip and I were talking, and I looked up at him, all six-feet-three of him, and saw an incredibly attractive, confident, kind man standing before me. It was like I woke up and saw what was in front of me the whole time. But it was too late. Phillip had moved on and was no longer interested. He was still kind as we talked, telling me he had prayed for me for four years, but that things were different now. I remember looking up at him as he said those words. I thought, *Wow, he prayed for me for four years? I've never prayed for anyone more than once or twice.* I'll never forget that. I still think of it today and am inspired to pray for others faithfully. I'll also never forget the feeling I had when I realized the opportunity to be with him was gone.

I held out a little hope for a while—after all, he wasn't married yet. One summer, I went to church and sat next to him. He was sitting with his new girlfriend and he took her hand and pulled it over to me and said, "Look Liz, we're engaged!" My heart sank. I'm sure it was all over my face, but I tried to be excited for him. She was a lovely girl, and I was happy for them, as much as I could be.

I don't know if Phillip ever loved me. I know he liked and cared for me. But I'll always refer to him as "the one that got away." Because I let him get away. Because I couldn't see what was in front of me. Phillip was the best of the men I loved and didn't marry.

I'm still friends with him and his wife. Last summer when his oldest daughter got married, I had the privilege of seeing him again. I hadn't seen him in twenty years. Phillip has nine beautiful, blonde children with his wife. Yes, nine. He definitely married the right girl.

I know now I wasn't the best for Phillip, even though at one time I thought he was the best for me. His wife is the best for Phillip and I am the best for my husband. I don't have any illusions about that; it's simply the truth. He was and is one of the best men I know, stellar in every way. I'm better for having known him, and I'll always love him in some way. My husband knows that and is enough of a man to handle it. After all, he met him last summer at the wedding and after a few conversations, understands why. It's not really debatable; Phillip is an extraordinary person.

Jay: Chemistry

I met Jay when I was twenty-one and working a second job to pay my way through college. Jay was what you would call "a tall drink of water." He was six-foot-five with dark brown hair and brown eyes. He was a man's man, quiet and strong. He couldn't look me in the eyes for too long without turning away. The chemistry was palpable. I'd never felt anything like it before. I didn't know what to do with all that energy. I was drawn to him, so much so that I could barely get my work done. Needless to say, that job didn't last long. Jay was a little different than the other men I loved because he was the only one who wasn't a Christian. I was in too deep with feelings to care about that in the beginning. I thought what all naïve, young people think: *I can win him over.*

Jay looked at me the way a woman longs to be looked at—like she's the most beautiful woman he's ever seen. He adored me. He thought I was funny and smart and sweet. He also didn't think I needed to lose weight, and always wondered why I was so obsessed with it. The power this kind of acceptance has over a woman is deep. To be loved and seen for who you really are, to be desired for your beauty, as you are, not thinner, or younger, or prettier. It's intoxicating.

Jay and I didn't stay together for many reasons, the least of which being he wasn't the best for me and he knew it. He let me go. He actually gently pushed me away, even after I kept coming back to him to feel the comfort of his arms again. He wanted me and I wanted him, but wanting someone isn't enough. Chemistry was the most powerful thing we had in common, and chemistry isn't what you build a life on.

I kept in touch with him for about twelve years, always going back to him in my mind as the one to compare all others to in terms of that elusive chemistry feeling. When I was about thirty-three, I knew if I wanted to move on and meet a man I could marry, I had to let him go and never contact him again. I've told my husband about him and about the chemistry we shared. I told him because I want him to know me. All of me. I also want him to be aware that I should probably never be in the same room with Jay again because those feelings could come back up. I want him to know so neither of us is caught off guard. It's highly unlikely I'll ever see him again, but you never know.

I think about him from time to time. When the movie *The Notebook* came out, I left the theater crying and thinking of him. That's definitely the kind of crazy chemistry we had. In that sense, he was the great love of my life. But in every other sense, he was just the first. It's still painful if I think about it sometimes. But I don't regret not marrying Jay. I have true love in my husband.

John: Friendship

I met John when I was twenty-three and living in West Palm Beach. I was hanging out with a bunch of people he knew from high school, and we ended up becoming friends. He lived in Tallahassee but was from West Palm Beach. John was an intense, charismatic, troubled, Catholic, Italian American. We had a lot of things in common: a complicated and difficult childhood, a desire for purpose, meaning, and spirituality in our lives, and we also liked to have fun—lots and lots of fun.

John wasn't someone I really "dated," though. In truth, in the beginning he was someone I was attracted to. I didn't know what to do with that attraction. I didn't understand it. It was more of a soul connection, but I mistook it for more. He was attractive and certainly good looking by anyone's standards. We did what I think a lot of people do who don't know what to do with attraction. We acted on it physically, and once that ran its course, we became friends. We should have directed our attraction better and limited our connection to friendship only. But we were both a little reckless and searching for something.

John was a character in every sense of the word. He was mischievous and ornery and witty and smart. He was spiritual and analytical and troubled and difficult. He wasn't always kind to me, but he was always fascinating. I didn't know I needed someone kind; I just wanted someone with passion. John certainly had that, though it was misdirected.

After we stopped being involved romantically, John and I developed a deep, soul friendship. He encouraged me to pursue greater things than I would have pursued on my own. John is the friend who convinced me to quit my job in West Palm Beach and move to Tallahassee to finish my degree at Florida State University. I knew instantly it was the right move. It would be six years before I would graduate, but I did it. I'm not sure I would have if it weren't for John. He saw potential in me when I couldn't see it in myself. He worked his way through college and made something of himself, despite his troubled family background. He inspired me to do the same. I would end up being friends with him for more than ten years before his untimely death at thirty-seven. He died of unknown causes. He just stopped breathing. It was surreal, sad, and shocking.

I loved John. I would have married him if he had asked, and then I would have been a thirty-three year old widow, so in some ways I'm thankful he didn't. John loved me the best he could, but he also knew he wasn't right for me. So he pledged to become the best friend he could to me, something that might surprise those who knew him. He used to send me encouraging cards when I was still living in West Palm Beach. To most, he was a "rough around the edges" guy, but I saw his tenderness beneath all the rough edges. Sometimes angry people really are like beaten dogs. They bark because they're scared. John was a powerful force in my life. He brought me a lot of pain and a lot of joy. He was a good friend. I miss him. I'm thankful for him. And I'm glad he's finally at rest.

Sean: Kindness

I met Sean when I was about twenty-seven. We met at church, where I always wanted to meet someone, especially someone I might marry. Sean was five years younger than me, but had such bravado you'd never know it. He was tall and thin with blonde hair and blue-green eyes. We were friends at first and didn't spend much time together until we went on a mission trip to Mexico for two weeks. It was a great trip and, as with most short-term mission trips, we spent a lot of time bonding with the team.

When we got back, we got together regularly to try and keep the spirit of what we had in Mexico. We got to know each other more, and one day it became apparent he was interested in me. At first, I was dismissive because of his age. I tried to hold firm in my position that while I liked him, he was too young for me. He claimed I was being ageist and closed-minded. Those words and his overall manner and persistence worked, and we began dating. In fact, I think we spent every day together for the next nine months. We had a lot in common—we had chemistry, we had friendship, and we had spirituality. Something was off, though, but I couldn't put my finger on it. I kept going back to the age thing, which completely frustrated him. I loved him, I did. I simply couldn't see marrying him, even though a big part of me wanted to. I had a deep knowing that I couldn't shake. He wasn't going to be my husband. Someone else was better suited for him. Someone else would be better suited for me. It was hard to explain; it was a certainty I had. In spite of this, it was still hard for me to move on.

He was wonderful to me. He was the most romantic person I'd ever dated. He wrote me poems, sang to me as he played his guitar, and cooked me dinner.

I felt he would have done anything for me and wanted the best for me. He was my best friend. That's why it was so hard when things finally ended. Since I'd spent so much time with him the past year, I didn't have many other close friends. When we broke up, I was incredibly lonely.

Sean would go on to meet his wife the following year, not long after we broke up. Even though I was the one who ended things, I still wasn't over him when he began dating her. I'll never forget talking with him on the phone as he told me about her. I was kind of in shock: *Wait, I don't understand, I thought you loved me and wanted to marry me? How can you be over me so soon?* I didn't understand how people can differ in this capacity.

Sean married his wife the following year. They're still together almost twenty years later. They've got three beautiful children and couldn't be more perfect for each other. She has been gracious to allow Sean and me to remain friends, and she and I have become friends ourselves. A few years ago, I had the opportunity to introduce my husband to them both, and we all shared a good meal together with some other mutual friends and their kids. I'm grateful to still know him and see him doing well.

He became the man he was meant to be, with the woman he was meant to be with. I'm glad I didn't override my instincts and try to keep him for myself. What a selfish act that would have been. Now I get to watch as he flourishes and loves his own family; that has been a gift to me. I'm thankful for Sean. I know I can always count on him to pray for me and my husband. They actually have a lot in common, even their giant red beards. Sean is a good man and I'm glad he's in my life.

———————

All these men were loves in my life. I made terrible choices through the years, looking for love and acceptance. These men were exceptions. I love hearing stories from people who were high school sweethearts and still together today. I often wonder what it would be like to have loved only one man. I certainly wish I had given my body to only one man. But I don't regret giving my heart. Some people might differ with me here. I say give your heart, in everything you do and to everyone you meet—not all of your heart, but as much as you can, even if it breaks a few times. It will heal, and so will you.

19

BEING MARRIED: LEARNING LOVE

As I've said before, I didn't get married until I was thirty-seven. By the time I finally got engaged, I thought I knew what love was and how to love someone. I'd been in love before, what could be so different? I soon discovered I knew more about being single, being in romantic love, and being in short-term relationships than I did about real love. I hadn't dated anyone longer than nine months. I never even made it through the infatuation period!

When I was young, I presumed I understood something—in this case love—if I'd read about it, heard about it, or observed it. Observing other people love someone may be as close as it gets to understanding, but it still doesn't replace firsthand experience. I thought I was clever asking all my invasive questions to whichever married friend would answer. But like everyone who gets married soon discovers, only marriage teaches you about marriage. Nothing else can.

As a child, I got my ideas about marriage by watching my friends and my closest sources. Marriage was what our parents did when they decided they wanted to have babies and live in a house together. As we grew up a little and started watching TV shows depicting married people, we learned from shows like *Happy Days* (if you were born in the '70s) that married people were simple-minded housewives married to men who wore ties and worked outside the home. At some point we realized these were fictional, one-dimensional characters and we started looking around at people in real life. We would never actually talk to our friends' parents—we would ask our friends what their parents were like. But teenagers generally only think in terms of how other people affect them, so the answers were short, skewed, and not very informative.

Like most people, I came to many of my conclusions and beliefs about marriage from watching and listening to my own parents. My parents were married for thirteen years and divorced when I was three years old. I can count on one hand the number of conversations I've had with each of them about marriage. I heard a few strong statements from my father about divorce, but very little about love or marriage. Occasionally when I was a teenager the subject would come up, and he would say things like, "God hates divorce," and "Your mother was selfish divorcing me and moving so far away; I never wanted the divorce." My mother rarely said anything about love or marriage, either. It seemed like most people from my parents' generation didn't talk about their personal lives or feelings. It just wasn't done. Certainly their parents didn't talk about it, so where would they have learned that talking about feelings might be a good idea?

My mother rarely spoke about my father, and when she did, she never spoke ill of him. I was too young at the time of the divorce to understand it. Later on I remember her saying, "Your father and I just didn't work out," and "I just couldn't take it anymore. I was very lonely and tired all the time, taking care of four children by myself." That all sounded reasonable enough.

I learned later, after further probing, that he wasn't a very good husband or father because he was rarely home. He wasn't there for the births of any of his children. He was always working. She said he was a good provider, but that's about it.

As I got a little older, I learned that my father had certain expectations when it came to marriage. He liked things a certain way, like home-cooked meals on the table every night and sex whenever he wanted it. We never talked about sex, so I didn't know what to make of this information. I did get the impression they never made love; perfunctory sex was more common. They weren't good friends, either. They shared very little conversation, activities, or hobbies. From what I can tell from their stories of how they met and why they decided to get married, their courtship was based on physical attraction and charm. He was a dance instructor at a ballroom dancing studio. "He literally swept me off my feet," she said.

I guess their story isn't all that different from many people growing up in the '50s and '60s; getting married and having kids was what you did. There didn't seem to be a lot of thought put into it—no compatibility testing, no psychological profiles, no premarital counseling. These things simply weren't part of the culture. I wonder if it would have made any difference for my parents. In our modern day, it still seems like most people continue to get married for these same reasons. Sometimes they have more information and still, often against their better judgment, they marry anyway. Physical attraction, loneliness, and the desire for a family are common reasons for marriage. With all the changes in our society, many of these basic drives still remain.

One of my former mentors is a marriage and family therapist. He described marriage as counterintuitive, meaning it's about being selfless and giving to another person when intuitively we're more designed to be selfish and serve ourselves. He also said something else I'll never forget. He talked about living "single-well and married-well," meaning if you couldn't live well as a single person, you weren't likely to live well as a married person. He was right. I didn't live well as a single person until the last few years before marriage. Fittingly, I didn't live well as a married person until well into my marriage.

Tim and I are now into our eleventh and best year of marriage. No words adequately express how grateful I am that we're still together and choosing to love each other. We are in our sweet spot, after fighting hard for it. In many ways, I feel like a different person than when we first married. My basic nature is still the same, but marriage has changed me for the better. I finally grew up and learned what love is. My husband wasn't the answer to all my problems. In fact, I inherited some new problems, as did he. But he was and is the person who keeps choosing to be for me in every way he can. I needed that kind of love, one that I could count on, one that I could trust. I needed it more than anything in the world.

The night before our wedding, I was peaceful. Of course I had no idea what I was getting into—does anyone? Would anyone get married if they knew all the changes that would inevitably come? I was peaceful because I kept thinking about my soon-to-be-husband's character. His character put my heart at ease. I saw in him, from the beginning, all the things that remain true today. Chemistry wanes. Character lasts.

My husband is genuinely kind. I needed someone kind more than anything. He's not critical or judgmental. I needed someone who wasn't always criticizing and judging me. I did that enough on my own. He's pure in heart. He has no guile and no pretense, my favorite quality in any person. He's completely trustworthy. I've never once felt I couldn't trust him. I'd never completely trusted any man before. He's honest to a fault. He doesn't lie, ever, for any reason or under any circumstances. It's comforting and stabilizing to know you will always be told the truth, even if it hurts.

He loves the truth. He loves learning. He loves the Bible and God and wants to do what's right more than anything. These are the reasons I married him. This is my husband. He's grounded and solid and steady and true. He doesn't change who he is or how he behaves based on his circumstances. It's one of my favorite things about him. Daily I see how his steady manner compliments me. I want that kind of balance. I want the differentness he brings. That wasn't always the case. Our differences almost drove an immovable wedge between us.

In our first years of marriage, our differences often drove me crazy. I couldn't see how they helped; all I saw was how different we were and it was isolating, not comforting. I also began to notice other things at work. I didn't realize it at first, but I was trying too hard to play the role of what I thought was a good Christian wife. I had an idea of what I should be like now that I was married. I got this idea from Christian culture, or rather the extreme fundamentalists within that culture. It wasn't altogether wrong or out of line with my desires, but it was restrictive, limited, and incomplete. I wanted to be a loving, gentle, kind, honorable, and helpful wife—nothing wrong with that. But I believed if I expressed my thoughts and feelings regularly or passionately, I would be seen as anything but gentle and helpful.

My husband had been married twice before. Both marriages were hostile and argumentative. It was almost as if he married the same woman twice. I didn't understand it. All I knew was I wanted to bring him a different kind of life, filled with peace, kindness, and gentle words. I wanted that for myself. While I hadn't been married before, I did grow up witnessing a lot of hostility in my father's and stepmom's marriage. I couldn't imagine ever being in that kind of marriage. And so I did what a lot of people do: I overcorrected. I went into marriage focused on what I *didn't* want. I didn't know how to ask for or produce what I *did* want.

I didn't know how to disagree without sounding argumentative. I didn't know how to be myself and be a wife at the same time. I was overcome by my fear of doing it wrong and my desire to do it right. I wasn't sure how to be honest or real and true to my vows at the same time.

I believed that if I said what I was feeling, I would be seen as discontent, ungrateful, and not Christlike. What I was feeling wasn't wrong or sinful or unkind in any way; I was simply lonely. Lonely in my marriage, the one place I thought loneliness would disappear. And I couldn't blame my husband. When you don't share your heart, you live in a prison of your own making.

He traveled for work four out of seven days a week, and every other weekend we had the kids. That meant we had a total of eight days a month alone together. At first, I thought it was great—no cooking and cleaning for more than half the week? That sounded amazing! I quickly realized the cost was greater than the benefit. I needed in-person time with my husband to get to know him more and to know myself more around him.

He had his own fears and desires about our new marriage. But being a rather cerebral and unemotional man, he didn't share his thoughts and feelings with me either. We both brought in our expectations of what marriage to each other would be like, and we both hid our newfound realizations neatly under the surface and didn't talk openly with each other. He didn't seem upset or disappointed or bothered in any noticeable way; he just seemed politely uninterested in me. He was never unkind or hostile. He was never picky about food or schedules or where to go or what to do. He was always grateful and always peaceable. It took me a long time to discover what was going on with me, and with him.

When the environment is generally peaceful, you feel you have no right to complain. I had married a hard-working, gentle, faithful, and kind man. He didn't lie, yell, cheat, drink excessively, spend too much money, or treat me disrespectfully in any way. So why did I begin to feel more like the cook and the maid who slept with the man living in the house? Why did I see less and less of my personality? Why did I quietly turn into someone I didn't even recognize? I wondered all these things as I suffered in quiet desperation as the days turned into months and months into years. When there was no connection, even the duties I willingly chose as a wife began to feel like paid obligations.

I was managing my uncomfortable feelings in the old familiar

EVER LIGHT AND DARK

way by baking (and eating) muffins and cakes I'd made "for the kids." Strangely, I was the only one gaining weight from this activity. While cake usually makes everything better, this time it was just making everything worse. As my waistline grew, so did my fears and hopeless thoughts. Something had to change. No more hiding. No more baking. No more being quiet and polite. I needed to get back to being myself. But first I needed to find my way back. I was lost again.

I started confessing my feelings to a friend and eventually began to get help in the form of counseling. I realized my story of feeling lonely in marriage wasn't unique. I stayed in counseling for a couple of years with the support of my husband. Although, in the beginning, I only shared with him that I needed help adjusting to my new life being married with children who weren't my own. That was certainly a reasonable request given our scenario. I didn't yet know how to share the most vulnerable part of what was going on with me. I didn't even understand it myself. I had become a sad housewife. I had dinner ready every night he was home, we had sex regularly, and this was all looking frighteningly similar to my parent's marriage.

Over time and through counseling, I was able to share with him, little by little, more of my feelings. It didn't always go over well. I still didn't know what I was doing or how to honestly communicate any of these emotions. We hung in there and kept moving forward. He was reluctant but eventually agreed to marriage counseling. We went to several different counselors over two years. He even agreed to attend a workshop with me in Seattle led by Dan Allender at The Seattle School of Theology and Psychology.

He continued to meet with his friends and pray about our marriage. I continued to meet with mine and do the same. However, while a lot was being worked on, still nothing was really changing. In fact, I was growing more hopeless, and my husband was growing tired of trying. We were finally at a crisis point.

So we agreed to separate. I didn't want a divorce; I didn't even want to separate. I was desperate for new life in our marriage. Some key things were about to happen that would change the course of our marriage for the better. One was picking up an old book written by Steve Brown of Key Life Ministries. Before he was famous, he was my pastor in Key Biscayne, Florida, in the '80s. His sermons changed my life, and twenty-five years later, one of his books would do the same.

He said people were always asking him to write a book on marriage, and he always refused. He said even though he'd been married for more than forty years, he didn't have enough material for a book because he only has one piece of advice: "Don't leave. If you leave, you'll never get to the joy." This was especially helpful to me because I know of little more to do in an uncomfortable situation than leave.

I don't think it's a coincidence that I happened to read his piece of advice during the most difficult period of my marriage. I was considering separation as a last-ditch effort. I didn't know what it would accomplish, if anything; I knew I had to do something different. When I read Steve's words, they affected me. I believed them. I didn't think our marriage was something I wanted to give up on, and I certainly didn't think my husband deserved to be given up on. I didn't want to leave for good; I just wanted a break from the tension and each other.

We met with a friend from church who helped us talk it through, what separation would look like, what it would mean. Through the next several days, my heart changed. I didn't want him to leave, and I didn't want to leave. We decided to stay and work it out, together. I was peaceful and relieved as we talked that first day. There was a glimmer of hope infused back into the relationship. It felt right. I loved him; there was no doubt about that. I wasn't sure how it was going to work out, but I wanted to try, and to try something different, together.

There's a memorable quote from the film *To the Wonder*[1], when the character Father Quintana says:

Emotions, they come and go like clouds. Love is not only a feeling. You feel your love has died? Perhaps it is waiting to be transformed into something higher. Awaken the divine presence which lives inside each man, each woman. Know each other in that love that never changes.

Those words have stayed with me ever since I first heard them. I say them as a prayer and a hope for my own marriage. Divine love is something I can believe in.

That was the beginning of a lot of changes for us. Six years later, Steve's words are truer now than ever. I didn't leave, we're on the other side, and there's so much joy in our relationship. There was a lot of work, tears, counseling, heated discussions, silence, tension. But slowly and surely it got better. We leaned toward each other instead of away. We didn't give up on each other and start over with someone new. We wanted to stay married to each other, and we had enough love and goodness between us to try.

What happened after we decided to stay together felt like divine intervention. I don't know what that means except to say we couldn't have done it on our own without spiritual help. I had a deep sense that I, not my husband, had to change and stay in my marriage. That deep sense was one of the things I felt saved our marriage. I had a deep knowing that I needed to change and do something different, from within my marriage.

This awareness happened first when I was sitting out on the back porch one day, looking up at the sky. I had a thought so clear, it was like someone was speaking to me. I knew, in the deepest part of me, as much as any human being can know, that the thought was from God. The thought was this:

You have to let your husband go. You have to leave his growth and development as a man and as a husband up to me and stop trying to change him. You have to work on yourself and leave him to me. You have to trust me with this. You have to let go. You have to stay, and then you have to let go.

Later that day as I waited for him to come home, I prayed for God to help me tell him what I felt. I wanted to have the right words, I wanted to tell him I was letting go. I did, and my husband heard me and received what I said. He appeared visibly relieved and optimistic. I wondered how long he must have been waiting to be set free from my unseen grip. I was relieved and peaceful too. Something changed and it has never changed back.

The counseling, workshops, and discussions weren't in vain. They aided in the formation of our new, more honest marriage. My husband changed too. My greatest desire was for him to be present with me. He knew there were problems, but avoided drawing near because he didn't know how to fix them. So he kept busy working and doing other things. He said from then on he would try showing up, without any answers, and see what happened. He decided this, on his own, without any "encouragement" from me. I noticed right away. He was present with me again in his thoughts, instead of thinking about work or other things while we were together. He began paying attention to me again, like when we were dating. He'd ask me questions, listen, and just sit with me. Most of the time it was only ten minutes, but he was fully present for those minutes, and my heart knew the difference.

Sometimes ten minutes of undivided attention can be the difference between feeling lonely in a marriage or not. In those first years, I wondered, *Do you see me? Do you love me?* Since this shift in our marriage took place, my husband chooses to show up, and by doing so, answers those questions with a resounding yes. I don't feel alone in my marriage anymore, and it's made all the difference. This choosing is the core of our love and marriage. One day, two people choose to love and honor each other for the rest of their lives. Every day after that, they make that choice again and again.

If I could, I would do two things differently: Always be myself, even while I'm growing and trying to be better. Don't try to "help" or "change" anyone else—specifically, my husband. Let him and everybody else be themselves and pray for their good.

I learned love in marriage. I am continuing to learn love, in all its forms and from its truest source, God, who has promised never to leave me. I am still learning, and it takes a lifetime. As for my choices, I choose God, I choose my husband, and I choose to stay and keep learning love.

20

BIOLOGICALLY CHILDLESS: A WEIGHTED DECISION

I decided not to have children in the same way most big decisions are made: through a number of small decisions over time.

In my mid-thirties, I met someone who was looking like he would be the man I would marry. We were dating long-distance, so we had to talk on the phone a lot. We were having one of our many get-to-know-you-deeper conversations, when he casually mentioned he'd had a vasectomy.

I was quiet for a few seconds, then said, "I'm gonna need a minute, can I call you back?" I took a few minutes to absorb what I'd found out, then called him back.

When I called back, the first thing he said was, "I'm sorry for just blurting that out. I know it's a big deal." Yes, yes it was a big deal.

We had a subsequent conversation on the topic in person. I remember details of that talk like it was yesterday. I can see where he was sitting on my loveseat in my single-girl apartment in Tallahassee. I remember standing for some reason. Was I protesting?

Was I preaching? Why was I standing? Was I trying to leave? Did my body know something I didn't?

After he left, for the next few hours, days, weeks, I had to consider a seemingly impossible decision. Do I pass over the man I want to marry in hopes of meeting someone else I could possibly have a child with?

Other questions soon followed. What if I can't have children anyway? How much do I really want a child or children? What if I never meet someone else I want to marry? Maybe we can adopt? Maybe he can have a vasectomy reversal? Maybe I'm not supposed to have children? He already has five children—maybe he doesn't want more? He's willing to have the surgery or adopt, but is that a good path for us? For me?

In my twenties I was sure I didn't want children. My siblings and I had a rough childhood and hadn't stayed close. There were no Hallmark moments to remember. I'd seen too much. My parents, even at their best, seemed burdened by us. At their worst, they made decisions that had devastating consequences for all of us. I didn't want to take the chance of doing the same with children of my own. I didn't want to unintentionally hurt them. I was sure I didn't want children, really sure, for an entire decade.

Then I turned thirty and some kind of pregnancy or mothering hormone kicked in. I couldn't imagine *not* having a baby. Babies appeared everywhere, and I made eye contact with every one of them. They seemed as delighted in me as I was in them. So I changed my mind. I now wanted to have a child. Just one. A boy. Then I changed my mind again. Just one. A girl.

Now we return to the part of the story where I've met my husband, and I'm making the impossible decision. You guessed it—I chose marriage with the possibility of no biological children. I was resolute and peaceful about it. It was a weighted decision.

Fast forward to year two of marriage. New questions arose as two became one and grew more in love. The vision of creating a little person who was a few parts him and a few parts me began to grow stronger.

Then those pesky questions returned. Vasectomy reversal surgery, seriously? How bad do I really want this? It might not even work. I am now almost thirty-nine—many more risks are involved. My stepson has Down Syndrome. He's very sweet, but communicating with him beyond a toddler level is extremely difficult. Could I handle that with my own child? Perhaps, but do I want to volunteer for it? I have some physical problems that will make pregnancy even more challenging—a bad back, a tilted pelvis, and a good amount of extra weight, even pre-pregnancy.

I thought, let's take our time and think about this decision a little more. But wait, I'm thirty-nine; I don't have a lot of time!

Another decision was made. No surgery. Therefore no biological children. Okay, this was going to be okay. This was our life. It was full and full of love. We were good.

A few years later, I started thinking about adopting a baby. I had completed a second year of counseling and felt new life springing up inside me. I dreamed of a baby of my own, but I couldn't see his or her face. I had friends encouraging the idea.

But I also was aware that this "new life" in me could be new healing and not longing for a baby. So I thought about it for a few months. More serious considerations, more questions, more doubts. Eventually, I realized that what was springing up in me was exactly what I had sensed—healing and new life. As crazy as it sounds I realized that I *was the baby* who needed nurturing.

I know that may sound like a bunch of self-help mumbo-jumbo, but it's the truth. It was time to care for myself in a new way, a gentle and kind way, the way you would a newborn baby. Peace set in and decision number three was made: no adoption.

I realize that peace doesn't mean the absence of pain; it means peace *in* the pain. Many days I felt free, settled, and calm, almost relieved at times. Other days, a tinge of sadness would appear, and I would second-guess my decision for a while, then return to peace.

As I moved through the next few years of life, I watched close friends having and raising children. I noticed several things. I saw how my friends, two in particular, softened and grew in gentleness. I saw how becoming mothers made them more calm and grounded in ways I hadn't seen before. I saw love in action as they cared and worried and fussed and laughed with their kids.

A surprising grief began to surface in me. A deep sadness I wasn't sure would ever leave me. I put words to that grief and strangely, it made it bearable.

I'm a woman, biologically made to bear children, and I won't bear any. I won't ever look into my child's eyes and see myself or my husband. I won't ever know the power of another human growing inside my body. I won't understand God's love for me, in that particular way, because I didn't create someone in love, for love. Other women will begin pitying me instead of admiring me. I will be isolated from my friends who are mothers because they'll think I won't understand, and maybe I won't.

These were intense thoughts and feelings. They had the power to take me down if I let them. Fortunately, the reward of counseling kicked in and I realized something.

This is grief.

I was surprised by it, thinking my desire for children wasn't that strong, but grief was there all the same. I started to let myself feel sad whenever it would come over me. It took about a year to move through grief entirely, but I did move through it and got to the other side.

I'm not deeply saddened by this decision anymore. It's some-thing always with me, kind of like a surgery scar. It doesn't hurt anymore; it's just a reminder that something painful took place and has since healed.

I am still a mother of sorts, and I do mother throughout my days. I mother my stepchildren, of course, and also my friends' kids, and sometimes my friends need a little motherly kind of love. I can't help but mother sometimes; it's in my design. At our best, we will mother those who need mothering. The recipients might not look like us, but sometimes people are in our lives because they need someone to love them like a mother would. Because we all need a mother's kind of love.

A certain kind of freedom came over me once I settled down deep into the life I'd chosen. A kind of calm was the new normal, as well as the beginnings of excitement about what the future could hold for us now. All the questions I asked in grief were about what I wouldn't have and what I would miss out on. I had to heal to think about all I would have.

You know those gratitude exercises where you write down everything you're thankful for? I'm a little reluctant to do those because it seems like a consolation prize for what you wanted to happen. I am grateful for many things. In some ways, I have the kind of life I never knew I always wanted. But life is also hard for me, and I suffer in ways I hoped I never would. Do I wonder what life would be like if I'd had a child? Of course. Is it helpful to spend a lot of time in wonderland? Not really.

I do think about how I'm able to notice things I wouldn't other-wise notice if I were raising a child at home. There's a kind of quiet mental space to my days that is my prized possession. Every mother I know loves her children and wouldn't trade them for the world, but she would also possibly sell everything she owns to have a few hours of this kind of quiet every day.

Comparison has never served me well, especially when thinking about my friends with kids. I used to drive myself crazy wondering if they secretly hated me for not being tired all the time. I often felt guilty around them and made self-deprecating comments, apologizing for my life. I hated that I felt the need to do that. Comparison and overthinking has stolen precious time from me. And it's really hard to stop. It's like a hamster on a wheel, running and going nowhere.

I've changed the way I think about those kinds of things now. The hamster isn't dead, but he's seriously injured. Life with my friends is less complicated. I enjoy them more. I help when I can and then I go about living my life.

Every day I try to remind myself what's true and be right where I am. In some ways my days are different from most of my friends; in other ways, they're much the same. They aren't without challenges or problems; they're just different challenges and problems. I cook and clean and run errands and scrub bathrooms like they do. But the pace of most of my days is different from most people in my season of life. The pace itself is gentle and free. This is a freedom I don't take for granted. I honor my mom friends by appreciating my life, not feeling guilty for it.

The world seems to be getting louder and more complicated every day. My response has been to get quieter and simplify. It feels like the best thing I can do. I try to take in simple pleasures as often as I can, like looking up at the sky, and paying attention to some of my favorite sounds: the wind, the waterfall in the backyard, the soft snoring of the dog. Sometimes a whiskey sour or a glass of good wine at the end of the week is celebration. Most of the time, just being still and thinking about what's truly good and pure and simple fills me. I'm thankful. I am. I'm finally free of many things. Heartache and pain have been my constant companions for a long time. I know they won't ever completely leave me as long as I'm alive, but right now I'm as free as I've ever been, and besides being loved, is there anything greater than that?

21

STEPMOM: ON HAVING ONE

My father remarried less than six months after my mother divorced him and left with two of their four children. My stepmother walked into a less than ideal situation. Yes, she chose to marry a recently divorced man with two children, but she couldn't have known the challenges she would face in trying to care for someone else's kids. I didn't live with my father at the beginning of their marriage, so I can't speak to what it was like growing up in their home, but I know it wasn't easy for my brother, sister, or my stepmother. I heard stories of physical abuse and alcoholism. I didn't witness these things firsthand, but I know from all of them that they happened, and I can speak to my experience of living with them when I was a teenager.

In the '80s movie *St. Elmo's Fire*, Demi Moore plays a character with a stepmother she regularly refers to as her "stepmonster." When I was in high school, I thought it was so funny and applicable that I started referring to my stepmother as my stepmonster. It made my friends laugh, and it made me feel better about having a difficult relationship with my stepmother. I never understood why she was irritable all the time. The overarching feeling I got from her was that I was in her way. She hated that I was in her house and was generally bothered by anything I said or did. I didn't understand then that it had little to do with me and almost everything to do with the situation she was in with my father.

When I came to live with my father and stepmother at age thirteen, it was under difficult circumstances for everyone. My mother had secretly arranged with my father to have me come live with them since I had become too much of a handful for her. I didn't know when I arrived that I wouldn't be returning to my mother's at the end of the summer as usual. I'm not sure, but I have a feeling my stepmother didn't have a say in the matter either. It was something she just had to deal with if she was going to stay married to my father.

I spent the first two and a half years in their house rebelling against everyone I could. I didn't make things easy on my stepmom, and apparently everything about me bothered her: the way I dressed, the way I talked, the way I did the dishes. She was furious at my mother, who had left two of her children and sent a third one to live with them. However, since she couldn't express her anger to my mother, who was 3,000 miles away in California, she expressed it in our house. I heard and felt her anger toward my mother, and, therefore, me. She probably tried to be kind to me at first, but my presence was a constant reminder of another woman's selfish choices. I understand now.

The next two or three years at home were largely comprised of me trying to stay out of the way, keeping busy at school and after-school sports. There were strange periods where it seemed she was trying to be kind to me, like on my sixteenth birthday. She threw me a party at a fancy restaurant we all loved. She had a cake made to look like me. She bought me a pink satin dress and took me to her salon, where she got me my first set of fake nails. She arranged for professional pictures to be taken and also bought me an expensive gold bracelet with my name on it. She said I could invite my boyfriend and a few other close friends. He wore a tux and everyone else dressed up like we were all going to prom. It was a really fun night and I did feel special.

I wish I could say my sixteenth birthday turned everything around for us and my junior and senior years were better. Unfortunately, the good times were over as soon as the cake was finished. We went back to being uncomfortable around each other, and I felt the same tension return. By the time I graduated high school, I was counting the days until I could leave for college. When I packed my car and headed for West Palm Beach, I looked in the rearview mirror and felt relief and satisfaction. I had made it through, and I never had to go back.

Of course I did return eventually, but not for three years. I don't remember where I spent those first three Christmases or Thanksgivings, but it wasn't at my father's house. Whenever I did return home, it was as uncomfortable and tense as in high school. Not much had changed. I would go on to graduate college and get married. She did not attend either event, because my mother was there. I knew it wasn't because she didn't want to celebrate me, but her refusal to attend for my sake kept us from being close for the next fifteen years.

After I had been married awhile, I went to visit my father, stepmother, brother, and sister. We had a nice dinner and then lunch the next day. After lunch, my stepmom pulled me aside and asked if she could talk to me privately. She then asked for my forgiveness for how she had treated me when I was growing up and explained it wasn't my fault. She was genuine, and it was easy to accept her apology. She explained it was about my mother, not me, and that it was a very difficult time for them. I understood. We have had a much better relationship since then. She also has been sober for more than ten years, which helps. She has been married to my father for forty-five years, which I know has not been an easy life. I'm glad she has found some peace. I don't see her and my father often, but when I do, it's pleasant, and for that I am grateful.

22

STEPMOM: ON BECOMING ONE

Stepmothering is sobering. It awakens you to the realities of the life you and others have chosen. Regardless of who's fault the divorce was or who did what to whom, the stepmother is now in a position of having to care for children who are not her own. The children are in an equally awkward position of having to at least respect this new, strange woman living with their father. It's awkward and uncomfortable for everyone.

I became a stepmother when I married my husband the summer of 2007. I was thirty-seven. His daughter was eight and his son was five. They lived with their mother in the same town about five minutes away. My husband also has three older children who were grown by the time we married and all lived in Colorado. I'm not really their stepmother except on paper. They are always polite and respectful when I have seen them a few times over the years. They aren't as close with their dad as he'd like. I wish we all could have developed more of a friendship, but distance, among other factors, has kept that from happening. Divorce and remarriage is difficult for everyone involved.

From the beginning, out of all the stepchildren the two

youngest children were the only ones who lived with us. My step-daughter is nineteen now and thriving in her sophomore year of college nearby. My stepson is sixteen, has Down Syndrome, and lives with his mother in Texas. They are both sweet-natured, gentle children. Everybody loves them. The ten years we had together were not without challenges, but they were nothing like the experiences with my stepmother. I knew it would be difficult to have a stepson with special needs, but I could only trust that my husband and I would face those challenges together. I was not as concerned about being a bad stepmom, especially to my stepdaughter, as I was about how my stepson would handle me as a stepmom. My husband assured me that he would do all the parenting and that I could do only what I was comfortable with. I went into my new role as open as possible. At the very least, I thought both of them could use a kind friend, given the hostile situation with their parents.

My husband had the kids part-time: every other weekend, one night a week, a month in the summer, and alternating holidays. I had lived with my stepmother full-time for five years, so in my mind being a part-time stepmom sounded more than doable. My husband was great with the kids when we were dating. He was gentle, patient, and loving. He listened to them, talked with them, and played with them for hours. I had never seen a father like that before. It was one of the reasons I married him. With those qualities in mind, I had little worries. We were in love, he was and is a wonderful, engaged, loving father, and the kids were sweet. How hard could it be?

Turns out it was a *tiny* bit harder than I thought it would be. Not because of the kids, but because of their mother, and the contentious relationship she maintained with their dad. The kids were kind, well-behaved, and respectful. If it had just been the kids and me trying to adjust to our new life together, I don't think we would have had a problem.

When I married my husband I had no idea how bad the relationship was with his ex-wife. I had heard a few comments and stories, but nothing that alarmed me. I assumed it was normal to have something negative to say about your ex—otherwise you'd probably still be married to that person. But my husband doesn't speak ill of people, even when they deserve it. He is also a mild-mannered, laid-back, nonemotional person, so when he did say something negative, it was relatively tame. He mentioned they didn't get along, of course, but he never said anything about her that gave me cause to worry. I felt blindsided by the reality of how painful the next ten years with her in our lives turned out to be. She seemed focused on making my husband's life and, in turn, my life, miserable. I tried to stay out of situations with her, but it was hard since we saw her weekly. Still, I was determined not to become the stereotypical new wife who complains about the ex-wife all the time. I tried to keep to myself and stay focused on building our new marriage and providing a good life for the kids. It proved harder than I expected.

I could write a whole book filled with story after story of the situations we went through with her over the next ten years. If you've gone through anything like this, you know how painful it is, and how nothing anyone can say makes it better. It is simply gut-wrenching, soul-sucking, life-draining drama. All I will say is that you should get all the support you can, learn and enforce good boundaries, and live your life peacefully, as much as it depends on you.

Your faith community will be a lifesaver. I don't know how anyone stays married in a blended family without the support of loving community. My husband and I also worked hard not to let his ex-wife come between us. We had difficult conversations and marriage counseling. We did the work. Part of becoming a healthy stepmom entails intentionally caring for your marriage and yourself so you can love the children well. Whenever I had the chance to take the focus off the drama his ex-wife was causing, I took it. I went for a walk, called friends, went to the gym, went for coffee, and went to counseling. I did everything I could to survive so that maybe one day we could thrive.

Stepmothering is different for every person and every family. It's complicated, but it doesn't have to be terrible, even if you have no control over someone else's destructive behavior. My experience from childhood helped me remember it's not the kids fault. They did not ask for this. It's hard for everyone involved, but the kids are the ones with the least amount of choice, and that makes all the difference. I understand what it's like not to have the choice of where you live and who takes care of you. My stepchildren had to deal with a new person they didn't know. They had to travel back and forth between houses. They had to try and stay out of the mess their parents caused. They needed a grown-up to help them with all this. I wanted to try. I had to learn to be sensitive to what these particular kids needed.

I was determined to be available for them, for whatever they needed and for however much of a relationship they wanted. I wouldn't force anything. I wouldn't require them to call me "Mom," like my stepmother did. I wouldn't take out my frustrations on them. I wouldn't expect much from them. I would be the adult in the relationship. I would carry as much of the burden for them as I could reasonably carry. I didn't love them when I married their father; I barely knew them. I would have to get to know them and learn how to love them, and they needed time to do the same. Each child is different, and these two were no exception.

Still, it wasn't easy for anyone. Besides dealing with a difficult ex-wife, the hardest part for me was not having them as babies to develop an emotional bond with them. By the time I came into their lives, my stepdaughter was a young lady and already attached and bonded with her own mother. My stepson was only five, but he was also too old to bond with in the way you might with an infant. For the first few years, I accepted this. It was normal not to have much of a bond with them. But after seven or eight years passed, there was still only a slight bond, and it was disappointing to me.

We all got along and enjoyed each other's company, but we weren't close. I wanted to be closer, but I wanted it to be natural. There isn't a whole lot of "natural" when it comes to step-parenting.

My stepdaughter knows I love her, and I know she loves me, but it is different than I would have thought. It is okay, though. Different isn't bad; it's just unexpected. I wanted her to know she had a friend in me if she wanted one. I don't think we had a chance to become close, though. Her mother wouldn't allow for that. I learned early on how difficult it was going to be. If I ever tried to take her to the movies or shopping and her mother found out about it, she would call during our visit and make her uncomfortable. She often yelled so loudly I could hear her through the phone. My stepdaughter hadn't done anything wrong. She was just trying to be a kid, live her life and not upset anyone. The pressure to handle all these parental relationships must have been unbearable at times. She handled it well, but I wish she didn't have to handle it at all.

In spite of these challenges, I never worry about her being happy or succeeding in life. I'm confident she will. She is gifted, and she is kind. She also wants to do what's right and wants to follow God more than anything. I don't believe you can go wrong with these qualities. Her dad and I have given her everything we could to support her dreams and make sure she knows she is loved. She is in college now and for all intents and purposes, an adult. I hope she remembers she is loved and that we will always be here for her.

As for my stepson, it's a bit more complicated. For all the same reasons things were difficult with his sister, they were even more difficult with him because of his special needs. I did not pretend to know how to parent him. I was a student from the beginning where he was concerned. I can be an emotional person, and he is emotional too. In the beginning, connecting with him was all about making him feel safe and cared for. That's what I wanted for both the kids in the beginning and throughout their time with us. I made concerted efforts to provide a calm, loving, safe, and healthy environment for them to grow up in.

My husband assumed the main responsibility for his son when he was with us, but I wanted to help if I could. I took care of him, fed him, played with him, changed his diapers, and even corrected him when he was being ornery. He responded well to me. I was firm but always gentle. He was comfortable with me. He thought I was funny, but seemed to know he couldn't manipulate me. I was probably more like a babysitter to him. He has special needs, but in many ways, he was like any other boy at that age, testing limits and looking for attention.

I had been married to their dad for five days when both kids came to live with us for a month. It was a rough start for all of us. We survived and lived to tell about it though. The next eight years of life with my stepson were a little better. Tim handled the potty-training most of the time, but that was never easy. Even more difficult than the potty-training, though, was the lack of development he was having in speaking and forming complete sentences. It has only slightly improved in the last eight years. He's still very sweet, but also very hard to understand.

At first, I was at a loss of how to begin trying to communicate with him. How was I going to relate to him, understand him, and care for him when he still couldn't form words properly, and he wouldn't be able to far into his teenage years? Except for the regular and adamant use of words he knew and used for food requests, I couldn't understand a thing he said. It frustrated me and made me angry and sad for him. I never took it out on him. It was not his fault. If I was frustrated, I would leave the room before getting upset with him. He was still the child, and he needed more help than he was getting. I learned over time how to communicate with him the best I could. Many times, a certain look or tone of voice worked. The rest of the time, hugs, music, food, and laughter were what we shared. He loved riding in the car with me and singing. I also sang to him at breakfast; being sung to was his favorite.

I've been told and believe that parenting is the hardest job in the world. If it weren't, everyone would be doing an amazing job at it, right? Parenting is definitely the most important job I can think of, next to teaching. I chose not to have biological children. I chose to become a stepparent. I own my choices. Maybe that's something we can do for our kids; take responsibility for our choices. It sounds like a simple thing, but the parents I've seen do the most damage are the ones who blame everyone else for their problems. Think of how our society would change with a little accountability. I love my stepkids. It's a different kind of love than I thought it would be, but it is genuine. It's awkward and tender and messy and holy, all at the same time.

Early on in my new role I asked God to give me a supernatural love for his son and daughter. It wasn't that I lacked affection for them—I liked them very much—but I lacked the natural love of being their mother, because I wasn't. I recognized the only way I could love them well was by the grace of God. I have no other advice for would-be stepmoms except to throw yourself on the mercy of God to get through each day with a measure of grace and goodness. It is the very best choice you'll make in parenting.

23

PARENTING: WHAT I WISH MY
PARENTS HAD TAUGHT ME

My strong feelings about parenting come from the heart of a child rather than the mind of a parenting expert. As a stepmom for the last ten years, I have learned some valuable lessons. I have learned that my ability to help or parent my stepchildren is limited. After all, they have two parents already. So my hands often feel tied. I try to stay open and available. I try not to be the stereotypical negative stepmother. I have loved my stepchildren the best I can and the most I have been allowed.

Much of what I believe about parenting has been learned by watching others. I'm not giving parenting tips, nor am I claiming to be an expert; no good parent would tell you he or she is an expert. In fact, the best parents I know say the least and do the most. But for what it's worth, here are a few things I wish my parents had taught me. Like any child, I didn't know how much I needed these things at the time. I would only realize their value later as an adult, when negative consequences forced me to look into why my life wasn't working well. While I could still implement these things as an adult, it was much more difficult to put them into practice. If I had known how to ask for these things when I was a child, I would have said:

Help Me Learn Delayed Gratification

It will be the single greatest act of kindness you can do for me. It will help me in every area of life, from finances to relationships, to physical, emotional, and mental health. Allow me to be bored. Let me learn how to deal with the discomfort I feel when I'm bored. I will settle into it and become more creative, patient, and self-motivated. Give me the gift of boundaries, limits, and guidelines, and when I don't follow them, discipline me. Discipline and limits make me feel safe. I need them; I become anxious and confused without them.

Allow Me to Fail at Little Things

Allow me to experience the consequences of defying your advice firsthand. I will likely remember it better the next time. For example, going out for a walk without a coat and getting cold, or eating dessert before dinner and then not being hungry. An example of allowing me to fail in a big way: giving me all the trust fund money my freshman year of college and hoping my eighteen-year-old self makes good financial decisions without any experience, knowledge, or parental modeling. Yes, this actually happened. I was in a car accident when I was seventeen. Two of my vertebrae were fractured when a milk truck ran a red light and hit the car I was in. My father sued the company, and we got about $16,000 after attorney fees. I asked him for the money when I turned eighteen, and he simply gave it to me. I bought a used car ($4,000), paid for a year of private college ($8,000), and blew the rest ($4,000) on going out with my friends, sushi, and new shoes. I ended up graduating with $18,000 of student loan debt that could have been avoided altogether with a little planning and parental guidance (twenty years ago, eighteen thousand dollars in debt was a lot).

Listen to Me When I Come to You with a Problem

Try not to fix my problem too quickly. Encourage me to come up with a solution rather than depend on you for one. Teach me the art of brainstorming without judgment. I never even knew this concept existed until I was well into my thirties. This can be especially helpful for fathers when talking to their daughters. Often, we want you to listen to us. We want to know we are loved by you. We may even come to you with a problem we already know the answer to just to have your attention, just to be in relationship with you. It also helps us to become more solution-oriented than fixated on the problem when you take the time to brainstorm with us, even if you know the best answer already.

There is no lack of information on the subject of parenting. We are inundated with so-called parenting experts giving advice. Honesty, accountability, and self-control however, are not as prevalent, and they seem like a good place to start.

SEEKING LIGHT

24

COUNSELING: AN OUTDATED TABOO

I'm not sure why people are still reluctant, ashamed, scared, or downright opposed to getting counseling (or "therapy," if you're old-school). I know our parents and their parents and their parents before them didn't get counseling, but isn't that telling? How different would their quality of life and the lives of their children have been with a little help in this area?

Actually, I get it. I still hesitate to tell people I've had years of counseling. I wonder whether they'll think I have serious mental problems and label me as some kind of deranged or damaged person they should avoid. No one wants to be labeled. No one wants to be thought of as weak. But after listening to many different types of people over the years, weak is the last word that comes to mind when I hear that someone was brave enough to go to counseling. In fact, some of the strongest, wisest, healthiest people I know have been or are currently in counseling. So why is it so hard to believe counseling is a good thing? It can be life-changing—especially if you have a professional, gifted counselor.

In my experience, not all counselors are gifted. Some are merely educated. If the counselor is merely educated, he or she may lack the necessary gifts of empathy, wisdom, and discernment. Maybe that's where some of counseling's bad rap comes from: too many bad experiences with merely educated counselors. Yet I suspect it's also because of the stigma that still surrounds the profession.

My Experience with Nonclinical Depression

What is nonclinical depression, and is it even a real thing? I mean, you're either depressed or you're not, right? That's what I used to think. I sought medical advice and was not diagnosed as clinically depressed, so I assumed I was overly sensitive, contemplative, or a little more emotional than most people. While some of that may be true, nonclinical depression is real.

Nonclinical depression is defined as: "A normal reaction to painful life events and/or physical, mental, and emotional stress."[1] The most important part of that definition, for me, is that it's a *normal* reaction. Because of painful life events, my brain is wired for sadness, worry, mistrust, fear, and negative thinking. I used to regularly wake up with a dark cloud, heavy fog, or gloomy feeling. Thankfully, that feeling is not consistent for more than a few days and therefore does not qualify for major depressive disorder. I am simply responding to painful life events and stress, and there are intentional things I can do to combat that stress and have a better quality of life.

I've seen doctors and professional therapists to inquire about clinical depression, especially since mental health issues run in my family. Each confirmed I do not have clinical depression or any other kind of mental illness. I used to live in fear that I would wake up one day and realize I had inherited a mental illness. It hasn't happened. It likely will never happen. What has happened is a lot of work and healing—mentally, emotionally, physically, and spiritually.

I have more questions about mental health than I have answers.

All I can tell you is how I've experienced mental health and some of the choices I've made to heal, the best I know how. I spent years, more than twenty years in fact, trying to heal myself through seminars, secular and Christian self-help books, church counselors, pastoral counseling, clinical counseling, acupuncture, praying, fasting, rededication or recommitment to faith values, and even hypnosis. While all of these methods can be helpful (some more than others), there is no absolute cure for nonclinical depression. My most trusted counselor and mentor suggests it's less like surviving and more like learning how to thrive—with the life, gifts, and challenges you've been given.

I know how to survive. I did that for most of my life. I was determined to survive and not be a victim. So I survived, but I also did not feel much of my life as it was going on. There's a great line from the movie *Postcards from the Edge* where the main character (played by Meryl Streep) says, "But that's the problem, I can't feel my life. I know that so much of it is good, but I just can't believe it."[2] The story is based on the actress Carrie Fisher's real life dealing with drug addiction in Hollywood. We all have ways of dealing with life and the pain that comes with being a human on this planet.

For most people in pain, the ever-popular behavioral choice is numbing, with anything and everything that will help ease the pain. I am no exception. This behavior helped me not to feel much of anything, good or bad. Different people use different methods of numbing: alcohol, drugs, sex, shopping, working too much, gossip, exercise, pornography, food, television, movies, books, social media, traveling, church overcommitment, and even spirituality. While none of these things in and of themselves are "bad" or unhealthy (with the exception of drugs), when I use them excessively or out of place, they create a substandard state of existence—lifeless and joyless.

I've heard these numbing tactics described as "shadow comforts." They can take on many forms since it's not what you do but why you do it. You can eat a piece of chocolate as a delicious gift and feel real comfort, or you can cram an entire chocolate bar in your mouth without even tasting it in a frantic attempt to soothe yourself. You can chat online for half an hour and be energized by community, or you can chat online for hours because you're avoiding talking to your partner about how angry he or she made you last night. Again, it's not what you do; it's why you do it.

When I first started paying nonjudgmental attention to these numbing behaviors, I began asking myself why I thought I was choosing to numb. For example, when Facebook started to explode and everyone was online posting and commenting nonstop, I would spend hours watching and scrolling, just like I used to do with channel surfing on TV. I felt better initially because, after all, I wasn't watching TV. Soon I realized I simply had replaced one numbing mechanism with another. As I nonjudgmentally asked myself why I was drawn to be online so much, the answer was clear: I was longing for connection with people.

Before Facebook was popular, I was living in a smaller town with many friends nearby. I was also involved in a small church of about two hundred people that met regularly during the week in each other's homes in addition to Sundays. I knew I had found something good in that little church and with those friends. I had no idea how good and how unique those connections were. It took me years to create something even close to that when I married and moved to Texas. But there are good people everywhere. I'm fortunate to have a close circle of faithful friends with whom I can talk and gather regularly.

Having no children of my own and not working outside the home in this season has changed my relational opportunities. I had no idea how those two demographics would limit my ability to connect. I believe community and authentic friendships to be lifelines for everyone, but especially for someone like me who struggles with nonclinical depression. I thrive on connection, especially among like-minded people. I wilt and spiral downward quickly when I'm isolated for too long.

Social media advances and availability made me question if instant connection online made me feel less lonely or more so. It's certainly no replacement for face-to-face connection, but I have enjoyed seeing the activity of my long-distance friends and family. It's been a better-than-nothing kind of connection when phone calls and visits simply aren't possible.

In addition to social isolation, lack of exercise and nutrition intensify my depression. I read a popular meme circulating on Instagram the other day that said, "Exercise is the most underused antidepressant, and food is the most overused anxiety drug." I couldn't agree more.

My childhood experiences changed the way my brain functioned and processed information. I was programmed to believe certain things about myself and others based on fear, worry, and anger. I didn't know how to express any of those things in a healthy way, so I was regularly, intermittently depressed. I later learned through professional counseling how to change the way I process information. I am now committed to regular exercise and a diet consisting mostly of whole foods, because I function better with these things. Being in community with people who share a strong faith is also critical for me. I need to be connected to other healthy people who are passionate about loving and serving others and growing in grace. This is my way of life. Choosing these life patterns is how I fight for mental health. I tell anyone who will listen: depression is real, and you need help to deal with it. There's no honor in going it alone.

I have heard my share of negative commentary about counseling from some Christian pastors and teachers. Comments in this vein usually suggest that counseling is selfish or self-serving, that too much introspection and "navel-gazing" is bad for you, and that your feelings and heart cannot be trusted. I understand the thinking behind these comments. I thought many of the same things. But while I do believe too much introspection and analysis is unhealthy, that doesn't mean that *all* introspection and analysis is bad. I also believe it's generally unwise to be tossed around and driven by our feelings and emotions, but I also believe that God has given us emotions for our benefit, to help us enjoy life. We are not meant to be emotionless robots.

The goal of counseling should be real, lasting change stemming from integration of emotional, mental, and spiritual health. For me, that means healing of damaged emotions from childhood experiences, connecting with God in my heart and mind, learning how to love myself because of that connection, and then learning how to get over myself so I can love others well. One of the best signs of good therapy is the ability to be largely free of self-obsession, absorption, and a need for attention. When you are grounded in love and acceptance based on who you are, not what you do, you're free to love and accept others and finally take the focus off yourself. That was the best part for me: getting healthy enough to get over myself.

Getting healthy took me a long time. The lies I believed about counseling took root early and were hard to uncover. I believed the preachers when they said all we needed was Jesus and that we couldn't trust our hearts. I spent many years skipping what I call "the middle step." I believe counseling is the middle step that can help people get from A to C. If "A" is the idea that we are broken and "C" is the idea that we need Christ, then "B" is the middle step to living a healthy and loving life with Christ and others. Good counseling can help us realize that *because* of Christ we are loved, accepted, and valuable, even with our brokenness. If we skip the middle step, we have an incomplete process.

I've also seen people slip into the habit of over-spiritualizing and over-complicating matters, something I believe wouldn't be as prevalent if they were to experience the freedom that comes from addressing hurts directly with empathy, compassion, and grace of a professional counselor. I don't understand the resistance to trying a different path. I do think it has a lot to do with what we've been exposed to and taught.

My exposure to counseling came at the early age of thirteen. I was what you would call a wild kid, someone who was acting out and out of control, at least as far as my parents were concerned. By the summer of my thirteenth year, I was experimenting with alcohol, drugs, and sex, with little to no regard for my parents or myself. My first introduction to a counselor was to a Christian woman my father sent me to. My father was ultra-religious, and when making me memorize Psalm 51 as punishment for my behavior didn't work, he felt professional help was necessary. To say that I did not respond well would be an understatement. I'm not sure that my time with her lasted more than a session or two, and I barely spoke to her. I felt punished, like my father thought I was crazy, and pushed into talking to a stranger about the most personal of things in my life. Let's just say it didn't work for me.

I wouldn't try counseling again for fifteen years. This time it was my choice. That factor alone made a huge difference. I was in my mid-twenties, and life was spiraling out of control. I had dropped out of college and was working full-time for an attorney. I was irritable, depressed, insecure, anxious, and in survival mode. I wasn't clinically depressed. I still got out of bed every day, showered, put on makeup, and went to work. But I was barely getting by.

During this time, I became involved in an inappropriate relationship with the attorney I worked for. I had been working for him for almost two years before anything inappropriate happened. It was one of the lowest points of my life. It went on for several weeks before I had the courage to make a change. I became irritable and short with clients, something I would never have allowed myself to do in the past. It was then that I made a phone call to someone for a counseling appointment.

In the privacy of the counselor's office, I told her what had happened, and we began a counseling relationship that would lead to significant healing (in addition to me deciding to quit my job).

147

Unless you've been in an abusive and manipulative relationship with someone who has power over you, you can't know what it's like to feel powerless to change or leave or tell someone. It's as if you are temporarily paralyzed. I'm certain that without the help of a counselor, I would have stayed in that situation much longer, with even more damage done.

This first adult experience I had with a gifted and educated counselor began my positive perception of all counselors. Over the next several years, I went to counseling, seminars, and spiritual renewal retreats, continuing to heal and grow. I then quit going to counseling after that for about eight years until I got married and life changed again. I had built a safe and loving network of friends and community, and had a lot of stability and support. When I married, I moved away from all my friends, my church family, and my job of ten years. Leaving my support system and marrying a man with young children brought new challenges. I quickly realized I needed to return to counseling and began looking for someone qualified.

Here's where we get to the part about the challenge of finding the right fit. The relationship you have with your counselor is critical. You need to feel like you can trust, respect, and tell this person anything. This kind of relationship is not a given just because you pick someone who's qualified, has the same faith background, or is the same gender. I began my search for a counselor the way I begin most things, logically. I looked for someone with the same faith background, then I based the rest of my decision on the first impression or vibe I got in our first meeting. I didn't care whether the counselor was a man or woman. What mattered to me was how I felt talking to him or her.

My first experience was awful. I went to a Christian counseling organization. The counselor was a man. The setting was perfectly comfortable, but I couldn't have been more put off by his style. I was uncomfortable right away. He was very cerebral and not warm or welcoming. He spoke of money almost immediately, and his overall manner was stoic. However, I wanted to give the process a chance, so I answered all his questions and stayed the full hour, even though I wanted to walk out after about ten minutes. By the end of the session, I was so frustrated and disappointed that I began to cry. Unfortunately, it wasn't because he had gotten through to my heart; it was because I cry instead of yell when I am frustrated and angry. He looked at me, perplexed, and said, "Why the tears?" It was a disaster.

Thankfully, I didn't give up looking for a better fit, although it would be another year before I tried again. The second attempt went more smoothly. A colleague had shared about her great experience in counseling and referred me to her counselor. His manner was much different. He was warm and welcoming, but also confident. He was funny and direct and wise. It was a great fit. I saw him for about a year. He helped me navigate the rough waters of a new marriage, instant family, and hostile ex-wife. He was a vital source of support and stability.

Over the next eight years, I would form two more counseling relationships with professional, educated, and gifted counselors. One of these women worked at the same office as the first counselor I saw many years before, the one that was not a good fit. I am glad I didn't rule out that counseling center because of my initial bad experience there, because this other counselor helped me in many ways. She was one of the counselors I saw when I was struggling in my new marriage. She helped me remember who I was before I married, and my personality started coming back to life. She was a strong, independent, Christian woman. She was wise and discerning and empathetic. My quality of life improved greatly with the help of her wise counsel.

My current counselor was an unexpected but treasured gift. She had all the qualities I looked for in a counselor but was even more gifted, intuitive, and kind. She is the most authentic person I have ever met. She is not only a licensed professional counselor, she is a strong Christian, devoted wife, and mother of four children.

She earned my trust and respect right away. I connected with her and felt I had met a kindred spirit. She seemed to get my heart, intentions, and desires to grow in a way no one had before. I believe she is God's gift to me and others, so that we can learn, grow, heal, and then give back to others from a place of health. There are no words to adequately express my gratitude for her. Through her wisdom, guidance, and love, I have become the person I've always wanted to be: still growing and learning, but with the knowledge that I am deeply loved and accepted. I share the things I've learned from her with anyone who will listen. My close circle of friends have been blessed by her words, too, as I share them often.

I can't emphasize this point enough: seek professional, gifted counselors if you want a better quality of life. You might spare your close friends from being worn out by situations they aren't equipped to handle. It's a fine line. As women, we want to help and lend a listening ear. However, there is no replacement for the unbiased counsel of a wise therapist. You might even save a few friendships along the way. Also, if you've read my story this far, you know I had a lot to overcome to get where I am. But overcoming isn't everything. There's much more to a healthy, purposeful, loving, peaceful life. There's living authentically and honestly in everything you do and with everyone you know. That is a life worth living and a life worth fighting for!

25

BODY IMAGE: A MISGUIDED OBSESSION

I spent the greater part of thirty years obsessing about the way my body looked.

I wasn't even aware of my body until I was about twelve years old. Until that age, I was free to enjoy myself and life in a childlike, unfettered way. Ironically, this is the way I think we're meant to live our *whole* lives.

I'm forty-eight now and have only enjoyed a few years of freedom from this fixation. Obsessions like this apparently take a long time to release. This focus on such a relatively unimportant part of my existence robbed me of more joy than almost anything else. It was the single worst repeated line of thinking I engaged in for more than three decades. I don't think all obsessions are bad. If we're obsessed about our families, a cause, the truth, then the fruit of these obsessions could yield something good. This body obsession only yielded pain and produced nothing of value. It was a misguided obsession.

Thankfully, though, when I was forty-five, I had an epiphany as I was talking with my counselor. I told her what she already knew but wanted me to discover on my own. One day after two years of therapy I told her, "I realized something the other day. No one who truly loves and cares for me is remotely concerned with what I look like." I knew this all at once, in the deepest part of my being. My closest friends, probably even my acquaintances, aren't the least bit concerned about it. They enjoy being with me, talking with me, laughing with me, and sharing their lives with me. They aren't thinking about how we would have a better friendship if I could just lose a few pounds. They aren't worried about my effectiveness as a Christian because of the size of my jeans. They aren't measuring my worth as a person by my ability to control my portions. I had been obsessing over my image as though those who love me were concerned with what I looked like. Those fears sound ridiculous now when said out loud, but when we're obsessed the ridiculous is normal.

Once I understood how my body image obsession had domi-nated my life, I had a choice to make. I could continue with this misguided obsession and two things would happen: I would not be present with God, my family, my friends—my greatest desires in life—and I would be denying myself and others the gift of my true self, which cannot be seen during obsession except in small moments and glimpses.

Or I could choose another way . . . . I could choose to stop feeding this obsession, and I could choose to focus on something else.

Where did this obsession with how my body looked come from? Besides the standard messages we receive from society, I have two pretty good ideas: Mom and Dad. Neither parent meant to do this, of course; it's likely how they were raised. Most of the compliments I got from my mother were about what I looked like. My father's comments definitely struck lower. "You're too beautiful to be overweight." "You have such a pretty face." "If you could just lose weight, you'd have everything."

In my thirties and still unmarried, the comments from my father were more targeted. "Well, honey, even Christian men are shallow, and nobody wants to marry someone fat." I remember thinking, *Wow, did he actually say that out loud?* He did. My father's acceptance, approval, and attention were directly linked to how I looked. He may not have intended this to be the case. Most girls I know want their father to adore them and tell them they are beautiful no matter what. I was no exception.

My mother was attractive and praised for her beauty, so I understand her actions more. She was repeating what she knew and valued. But however poorly my parents performed in this area, I can't blame my obsession with my body on them. At some point, I chose to continue this learned behavior.

As a teenager, before I started to become overweight, I learned my body was powerfully attractive to boys and men. I liked that feeling of power. I chose to indulge in that feeling. My parents had little to do with that. As I got older and experienced a tumultuous change in circumstances and surroundings, I began to slowly gain weight. My body changed from being healthy, curvy, and fit to heavy, chubby, and uncomfortable. I was still active, playing sports and going to the gym, but I was not healthy.

When I met John, I fell in love and wanted to secure his affections with my appearance. I was twenty-three. I managed to lose forty pounds over six months through drastic dieting (restricting myself to 900 calories a day) and working out excessively six days a week. I looked healthy, fit, and attractive. I was at a healthy weight and felt great physically. Unfortunately, my unhealthy methods could not be sustained, and I was unable to maintain the weight loss. Within four years, I gained back the forty pounds, plus an additional thirty. I was twenty-seven years old and at the highest weight of my life. For the next twenty years, I would gain and lose those same forty pounds over and over again. Can you imagine the insanity of that? Twenty years of obsessing about what I looked like, everything I ate, what new plan I could try to help me change and become a different person. It was exhausting and deflating.

I was not living my best life; I wasn't living much at all. I was distracted by my obsession and by my defeat. I was not living a life of love and service. When you're focused on yourself and your inadequacies, there's little time for others. A little gray cloud follows you wherever you go. I wasn't free to love people as I wanted to. Something had to change.

Some people might call me a quitter in this area. I would have to agree with them. I did quit. I quit being obsessed about the wrong things. I intentionally decided (and still decide every day) that the quest for a beautiful body is not more important than the quest for a beautiful heart. It just isn't. Health is important; body obsession is not.

My parents had it wrong and their parents and their parents before them. I'm stopping the cycle, even if it's just for me and my circle of friends. A life of body image obsession is a self-serving, vain, never-ending, peace-less life. I may never be fully satisfied with the way I look, but I am satisfied to not obsess about it anymore. I still strive to live a healthy lifestyle and take care of my body, but I can't obsess about appearance anymore. It's a bad habit I'm choosing to quit. I'm on to more interesting and important things. I lost many moments, days, months, and years. I don't want to lose any more. There are many more beautiful things in the world and so much beauty to create. I would like to spend my time creating more of that beauty.

26

FOOD & EXERCISE: LISTENING TO MY BODY

I am not an addict in the traditional sense. I've never been addicted to drugs, alcohol, or nicotine. I wouldn't even say I'm addicted to food, though I do love it. I definitely walk a fine line though on the verge of addict-like behaviors when it comes to some foods, and I may or may not have been known to put away a half loaf of fresh, warm bread when stressed, sad, lonely, or happy. There is clear evidence out there that I am an emotional eater.

That's not always a bad thing, since food has been given to us for our enjoyment as well as our nourishment. My husband happens to be one of those people who usually only eats when he is hungry and because he needs nutrition. If I hadn't introduced him to the art of fine dining, I don't know that he would care what he ate as long as it was healthy. These strange people eat to live, rather than live to eat. That's not me, for sure.

I've always known I was out of balance when it came to food, but I never saw it as a problem on the same level as a drug addiction. I thought: *At least I'm only hurting myself.* I even used to argue about this with my brother Michael, who has struggled with drug addiction for the past thirty years. Even though I still maintain that addictions to food and to drugs are not harmful in the same ways—after all, we can't live without food—I do wish I had been more compassionate toward my brother even when I didn't understand why he did what he did. Whether I struggle with drug addiction or not, I struggle with other things, and there's never an excuse to be judgmental or unkind.

I'm healthier now. I grew out of some of those unhealthy behaviors, like eating until I physically felt pain in my stomach. I still eat emotionally sometimes. Food is still my drug of choice. But it's losing its grip on me, slowly but surely. I started focusing on other things. I quit labeling food as "good" or "bad," and my behavior along with it. I try to be present and aware of my feelings and make good choices. Sometimes those choices mean warm, fresh bread and pasta. More often, those choices mean lots of veggies, fruits, lean protein, and healthy fats.

I have noticed a few things all the best eating plans have in common: regular exercise, water, and whole, fresh foods. The saying "you can't exercise your way out of bad nutrition" is something I totally believe. So I try to do the veggie, fruit, protein thing about 80 percent of the time. I just feel better when I do. That other 20 percent? Yep, that's for bread and pasta, and a little something sweet.

Food is meant to be enjoyed and savored. I've come full circle in my love/hate relationship with it. I know now that it's not good for me to use it like a drug. So I try not to. I don't always succeed, but thankfully, how and what I eat is not the most important thing about me.

Regarding exercise, there are all kinds of intellectual and spiritual reasons to exercise and take care of the body. Yes, the body is the temple of the Spirit, and we should honor that. Yes, we only have one body and need to take care of it. Yes, if we take care of our bodies they may last longer and work better. These are all valid reasons. But I also want to feel good when I do things like get up from a low chair or walk long flights of stairs. I want to be more comfortable in my clothes, less self-conscious in a bathing suit, and fit comfortably in airplane seats. I want to feel light and energetic, not heavy and tired. The bottom line: I want to feel good in body and mind.

I'm convinced the body was designed to work at its best when moving regularly. I'm not talking about never resting, because that's essential too. What I mean is that no matter how much lying around all day sounds like a fabulous idea, the reality is, my body starts to hurt after a few hours. My brain starts to feel foggy too.

So, after years of using exercise for all the wrong reasons, I finally started listening to my body and discovering what it needed and wanted. Feeling and functioning well is a great goal to have. My particular body likes to move frequently throughout the day. It also likes to rest, but enjoys it so much more after it has sufficiently moved.

Also, since I have struggled with nonclinical depression for most of my life, I wanted to explore ways to stabilize my mood naturally, if possible. I am not philosophically opposed to taking medications to help stabilize mood, but I wanted to see what a healthier diet and exercise would do for me first. It ended up being enough for me (each person is different!). I now think of exercise as nature's Prozac for me. I can wake up hating life and everyone around me, but by the end of a good workout, I can be smiling, laughing, and even ready to help others! I almost never feel like exercising, but I'm always glad I did afterwards.

I've played softball, basketball, volleyball, gymnastics, and tennis; I've tried dancing, yoga, step aerobics, free-weight lifting, group weight-lifting classes, Pilates, fitness dance, Tae-Bo, interval training, stairmaster, the elliptical, NordicTrack, swimming, water aerobics, bike riding, walking, and Zumba. No one could ever say I didn't give something a try! Weight lifting is by far my least favorite. Zumba is near the top of the list. Good music, friends, dancing, and calorie burning. As long as my knees hold out, I will be doing group dancing for exercise. I am a firm believer that if you don't enjoy doing an activity, it won't last—no matter how good it is for you.

Feeling good at this point in life has become my primary motivator, even more than health and physical appearance. Acceptance is a large part of feeling good. After a lifetime of rejecting my body, I now live in acceptance of it, as is. It wasn't easy or quick—it took almost thirty years. But now I realize that I simply cannot live an integrated life by rejecting such a huge part of me. I am thankful for what I've finally learned and accepted in this regard. I am glad I can now better listen to the messages my body sends me when it needs me to take better care of it.

27

HELPING OTHERS: THE WORST THANKSGIVING EVER

Y ou could say it was my fault. You could say I wasn't smart for trying to help him. You could even say you'd never let anything like that happen to you. But you never met Billy Dale Penny from Nowhere, Texas.

It was the Saturday after Thanksgiving. My husband and I just had the most relaxing, quiet holiday in ten years. My husband was on his way to a church meeting, and I decided to swing by the shopping center to look for a sweater. I didn't need one—I have plenty—but sometimes browsing turns to buying on a chilly, Texas afternoon. I pulled into the parking lot and immediately saw a man sitting on the curb with two dogs next to him. He had a sign that read, "Three dogs will work for food." I'm convinced I would have kept on walking if it weren't for those dogs.

I always feel sad, and a little angry, when homeless people keep dogs. How can they care for them, feed them, keep them safe? But I know the unconditional love of a dog, so there's nothing left to say. I'm not sure I could give them up if I had no one else in the world. When everyone else has grown tired of you, a dog will always love you.

So there he was, sitting on the curb, dressed in black jeans, boots, and a leather jacket, with leather skin to match. He wore sunglasses and had a long beard and long hair. He looked like a younger version of Willie Nelson, but more menacing.

I watched him from the car for a while, trying to get an idea of what he was up to. I called my husband to see what he thought about me talking to him and getting his story. His sign said he'd work for food, and it's hard to imagine the harm in giving someone food that is willing to work. Maybe there is no harm in it. I still don't know.

It was broad daylight in the middle of a wide-open parking lot near a Kohl's department store. I didn't feel unsafe; there were a lot of people around. I got out of my car and walked up to him. Before I could say anything, he saw me coming and said, "We might need a sweater in this weather today." Funny. I was just heading in to get one.

I asked him his dogs' names. Paloosa was a fluffy eight-month-old puppy who looked like my own dog. She was a Great Pyrenees mix, like my girl. Hercules was a three-year-old Chihuahua greyhound mix. He was an alpha, though, and kept showing the other dog who was boss. Then I remembered I hadn't asked the man his name yet. "I'm Elizabeth, what's your name?" Billy. Billy Dale Penny.

Now before I tell you the rest of the story, there's something you need to know about me. I've been burned before when trying to help people—not an uncommon story for people with my disposition. I've tried to see the best in people needing help, only to find out they were scamming me and others.

One time, when I was about twenty-three and living in an apartment in West Palm Beach, a young girl came up and asked for some blankets and food to help her grandmother who was sick. She didn't ask for money, so I didn't see the harm in it. I walked with her up to my apartment, let her come in, and gathered some supplies. She thanked me and left. The next day, the security guard for the building stopped me and told me he saw the girl I let in. He said to notify him immediately if she came back. She'd been wanted for conning her way into apartments to case the place for valuables, then reporting back to her gang so they could rob the place later. This was the first time I remember being shocked that anyone would ever do that. I was a different girl then—naïve, trusting, hopeful, altruistic.

Another time, a friend told me she had cancer when she didn't. She told everyone at church, and even her husband and son were fooled. She wouldn't let him go to the doctor with her because she was "private." He wanted to trust her, so he agreed. There were many times the whole church went to her house to pray for her and sing songs and visit. The whole time she was lying about having cancer. She was actually addicted to prescription drugs. No one suspected. Everyone believed her. Drugs will steal your integrity and your soul faster than anything in this world. They don't care who loves you or what you could lose. Watching my brother has taught me that.

Twenty years and twenty stories later, I'm not as trusting as I used to be. I don't start out thinking the best about people. I'm suspicious. I'm cynical. I have to fight against it every day. I'm not proud of it. I wish I could still say I believe the best about people until they prove me wrong. The truth is, more often than not, you have to prove that I'm wrong *not* to trust you. I'm not particularly gullible or naïve. I stay clear of people and situations that seem suspect. I'm not easily persuaded or manipulated into doing things for others. That's why what happened with Billy Dale Penny is unusual.

After a few nice-to-meet-yous and a round or two of untangle-the-dog-leashes, I got around to asking him how he came to be in the parking lot that day. He said he'd been living in a travel trailer and been in a terrible accident with a semitruck that totaled his trailer. He pointed to his current dwelling place parked a few spots back: a white pickup truck with a blue tarp in the shape of a tent over the back. He recently got a mattress and said that helped a lot because he hurt his back and neck in the accident, which was five months ago.

He'd been homeless, living in his truck, driving up and down the highway in Texas since then. He got the dogs three months before the accident, he said. Couldn't give them up, he said. "They saved my life more than once—they're like my family. No way I can give 'em up." I said I understood.

He said he'd been to several homeless shelters, but none of them would take him because of the dogs. There was one that would, but they required he be able to look for work and then work full-time. He said he couldn't do that because of his injuries. He was on disability, got a small monthly check, he said. "It's not enough to pay rent though, just barely gets me by. I always have plenty of dog food. Heck, I've even eaten that myself sometimes when there wasn't anything else." Whew. I couldn't imagine.

We talked a while longer, and I learned his mother was still living and in Oklahoma. "Why don't you stay with her?" I asked. "Well see, she's got my half-brother living with her, and he's a pervert preacher. I caught him watching gay porn when I came 'round the corner at church one time. I can't be around that." Again I said, "I can understand that." He went on to say he was a handyman by trade and just trying to make enough to buy a used trailer that he and the dogs could live in.

The whole time I talked with him, I was gathering information —not just words, but how he talked to me, his body language, and overall manner. He was not shifty or nervous, defensive or disre-spectful. He was calm and steady. He didn't appear to be high or drunk. He looked me right in the eye without fail, was polite, and not overly friendly.

It was Thanksgiving. I had been thinking all week about how I could help someone, even if it meant just sharing our meal. Most folks already had plans, and I hadn't looked into serving at any of our local soup kitchens like we'd done in the past. Now, it seemed like an opportunity to help someone was right in front of me.

He had some cards with his cell phone number printed on them, along with a picture of him and the dogs. "Three dogs will work for food. Head dog will do handyman work, windows, cleaning, and any special requests." I thought it was odd he had a nice cell phone, but thought maybe someone gave it to him and he got on a cheap plan. When you want to believe someone, it's not hard to come up with explanations for things.

I told him I'd talk to my husband and if he was alright with it, he could come over for an early dinner this afternoon before it turned dark, so he could see the yard work we needed done. I was hesitant to give him our address, of course, but I saw no way around it if we were going to give him handyman work to do on our house.

He came over on time, and we sat out back on the deck while he ate and the dogs played in the yard. We just listened, mostly, as he told more of his story. He continued to be polite and thanked me for the delicious meal. We played with the dogs and then planned for the next day. We gave him a heavy jacket since he said the one he had had been stolen. I'd been to the store earlier that day for groceries and bought an extra bag of apples, bananas, and protein bars, then threw in some dog biscuits when I got home. He thanked us kindly and said, "We'd best be going; me and the puppies turn in early these days."

We told him he could come back in the morning to start on some work. He showed up on time. It was cold, and I felt bad making him stay outside again for breakfast, so I talked with my husband about letting him in the house. We agreed it was fine. He came in and had a hot breakfast with us. We talked some more, and I asked if he had any children. He said he did have two daughters, but they weren't in touch. I asked him why, and he said, "Oh, you don't want to hear any stories that will make you cry." I said I could handle it and pushed a little more for the story. He wouldn't budge and stayed quiet. That was when I first started to become suspicious. What was the story there? Why couldn't he talk about it?

They went outside to work, and I headed to church. He helped my husband a little, but turned out not to be a good worker. In the middle of church I got a text from Billy. "Had to make a detour, tell the boss I'll be right back." Hmm, okay. An hour and a half later, I was out of church and back home. Still no Billy. I called him to see if he was okay. He answered and said, "Everything's alright, I just ran into an opportunity. It's actually a real blessing. I'll tell you about it when I get back. I'm on my way now."

Now I was definitely suspicious. He left in the middle of the job. He was gone for almost two hours. He had some story about what happened. And ten minutes later he showed back up . . . with a woman. I saw him through the front window and thought, *Oh brother, what do we have here?* I was hesitant as he approached the door and introduced her: "This is my long-lost girlfriend, Maria!" He proceeded to tell us that he had called his mother to check on her, like he does every day, and she told him that Maria had been looking for him, so he told his mother to have her call him. The rest of the story was a little muddy, especially the part about how exactly she happened to call right as he was out and about and just after my husband had given him $20 to buy a newspaper.

They came in the house and didn't stay long before I interrupted: "I think it might be better if we reschedule our work day for another time." He said okay, that would be great, so he could spend some time with Maria. They got the dogs and went on their way.

The next morning I began to get a bad feeling about him coming back. I called a friend to run the story by her. It became clear to me after talking it through with my friend that I needed to ask him not to come back. Before I could pick up the phone to contact him, Billy texted me. "I wondered if y'all lost faith in me because of my little detour yesterday." I replied, "Yes, we think it's best if you don't come back. Please respect our wishes. We tried to help and took a chance letting you into our home. It was inappropriate for you to bring someone we don't know back to our house. We wanted to help, but we're not comfortable with the situation any longer." I also included the contact information for two local shelters and work programs we had mentioned to him previously.

He immediately texted back. I wasn't 100 percent sure I was right about him and thought if he texted back and was decent and polite, maybe I'd been wrong. But he wasn't. His text said, "Understood, you deleted me so I'll delete you. You give up on a good man and his puppy dogs, baby girl. I lost someone I loved because of a mistake I made on Highway 20, so if you don't like her just delete her too. Done deal." Even though I had my answer now, his text made me angry and then sad. Was the whole experience a lie? Which parts of his story were true and which weren't? Who was this woman? Did he leave and go have a few beers with her with our twenty bucks? Were they planning this the whole time? We didn't know what to believe.

These days, I don't cry easily. I mean, I get choked up, but I'm talking about the kind of crying that's better described as sobbing. But after this was all over, I sat at my desk and cried. How could I have been so wrong? What was I thinking?

I felt bad the rest of the day. I tried to get the whole experience out of my system, to learn whatever I needed to, and move on. I had almost succeeded when the following day I woke up and typed his name into Google, hoping nothing would pop up. There it was, two lines down: Billy Dale Penny: Sex Offender.

My heart started pounding, and I couldn't move. My palms started sweating, and I almost quit breathing for a second. This isn't happening. I couldn't believe it. After I calmed down, I just kept thinking, "Why didn't it occur to me to Google his name *before* inviting him into our home?" It never even crossed my mind. I had become soft living in the suburbs of North Texas.

The Miami-version of me would have never let this happen. So many decades had passed since I had to worry about sexual predators, and so much healing had occurred. So much in fact that I didn't even look at strange men the same suspicious way. There is being naïve, being jaded, being healed, and then becoming wise. Apparently I needed a little more wisdom. I thought I was wise, but again, sometimes when you want to help your judgment can be clouded by the rose-colored glasses of your newfound freedom.

I gained my composure, called a friend, stopped by the church to talk to one of the priests, and went back home. As I was walking the dog, a Citizens Patrol SUV drove by. I flagged it down and reported everything I knew on Billy Dale. They were thorough and kind and took me seriously as they wrote down all the information. They said they would put everything in a report, and their supervisor would decide whether or not to send it to the police.

I walked back home and wished this had all been a bad dream that I could wake up from. It wasn't, though. It was real, and I wanted to learn from it and do something different next time. That's all we can really do: learn and do better next time.

So I came up with the following lessons learned from Billy Dale and my time at the end of Thanksgiving 2016. Doing good still matters; it's still the right thing. Having a kind heart that wants to help is still the way to go. Even the most discerning people can't always tell when someone is lying. Check the facts. Some people get so low in life that lying to a kind stranger is the least of their worries. Don't go out on your own. Join with an organization already doing good work helping the homeless and poor. They need our help and already have safeguards in place. It's not as glamorous or as immediately satisfying to give or contribute in a general way, or in small ways monthly, consistently. But it's still the best and safest way to give and help.

Keep a soft heart. Be wise. Fact-check. Ask questions. But keep a soft heart. Like my good friend Father Andrew said, "Cynicism has the power to be more toxic to your heart than anything else does. Be wise, then keep giving."

Father Andrew listened attentively that day as I told the story. He let me cry and get a little angry. He told me it's hard to know when people are lying, and he's not sure he can always tell either. He said not to spend too much time beating myself up and to get involved in something service-oriented again as soon as I could to fight the tendency to shut down. Then he prayed for me and for my husband. He prayed for Billy, too, that God would work in his life.

I don't know if Billy Dale Penny will ever change his ways, but I know one thing: I'm going to keep doing good and not let the cynic in my soul get the best of me. Because there's still good, there's still work to be done, and there are still people who need help and grace. And I need those things too.

28

DIVINE INTERVENTION: THE PIT
BULL ATTACK

L ife can change in an instant. People often say that but rarely pay attention until the change happens to them. For me, it was a regular Tuesday afternoon in suburbia. I had specifically planned to get my work done early so I could enjoy the random spring-like weather Texas was having in the middle of winter. After returning home and spending twenty minutes in the sun in the backyard while the dog played with her frisbee, I decided to take her for a walk. I was in sunshine bliss, living and soaking in the moment. I was unprepared for what happened next.

We ventured out on our regular path, winding in and out of the neighborhood streets and alleys. The weather was perfect, a slight breeze but not chilly, the sun in full view and blue sky with one or two cotton ball clouds. We stopped on a side road, and my dog sniffed some grass. All of a sudden I saw a shadow on the fence in front of me. Two seconds later, a pit bull had its jaws latched around my dog's neck and was thrashing from left to right.

It had come out of nowhere. It did not growl behind the fence or bark as it approached—it had snuck up on us like a stealth killer. I went into full panic mode. I had one singular thought for the next several minutes: *I must get this dog off my girl's neck or she will die in front of me.* I grabbed the pit bull's collar and tried to pull it off. I yelled, "Release!" like I'd heard a friend tell his pit bull before. I repeated the pulling and the screaming as I watched and listened to my dog cry and wail as loud as I'd ever heard. It's hard to describe the feeling I had as I listened to her. It was like someone poured hot liquid on my heart; my chest on fire and cold at the same time. I screamed for help, but no one was around.

Somehow I was able to pull them apart and keep hold of the pit bull's collar. I looked around to see where the dog could have come from, but saw no owner or yard with a gate open. I then made an almost fatal mistake: I let go of the collar and tried to shoo the pit bull away. I didn't know what else to do. It immediately turned around and bit my dog on the neck again, and wasn't letting go.

I lunged forward and fell to the ground as I grabbed his collar again and tried to separate them. I could see he wasn't budging. My instinct to protect my dog from certain death took over and I made a second questionable decision—I kept my right hand on the collar and put my left hand inside the jaws of the pit bull trying to pry it open and off my dog. Pulling on the collar wasn't working, and I had to do something. Still, nothing worked, and the reality was becoming clear that my dog might be killed. As I was on my knees wrestling this dog still attached to my dog's neck, I cried out in desperation, "God help me! God help me!" I kept thinking, *No good can come from my dog dying this way in front of me!* After I screamed for God to intervene, within seconds the pit bull released, and my dog bolted for home. It was an absolute miracle. There's no other explanation. I've been told over and over that pit bulls don't release once they lock their jaws on something.

I tried calling for my dog, but she was halfway home by then. There was no way I was letting go of the pit bull's collar this time. I stood there out of breath, holding tightly to its collar, looking around for anyone who would help. No one came. I began walking around to see if there was any gate open nearby, or if the owners were anywhere to be found. I walked around to the left of the fence where we had stopped to smell the grass earlier. As I turned the corner, I saw the gate open and swinging in the wind. I decided this had to be where it came from since no other gates around were open. I walked the dog up to the gate, released the collar, and he ran right in. I shut the gate, made sure it was properly latched, and ran home. I thought for a brief second, I sure hope that is the right house or someone got a dangerous dog put in their backyard. I would find out later it was indeed the correct house.

I ran into my neighbor coming home from work and asked if she would look for my dog who had run off after being attacked. I ran home, my hands and feet bloody from wrestling with the dog and scraping them on the concrete. My right shoulder was hurting, and I had trouble catching my breath. When I arrived home, my sweet dog was sitting at the back gate near the garage waiting for me. She had found her way home.

I brought her in the house, tried to examine her, and called the police, knowing they would contact animal control for me. I realized we were fortunate she was still alive, but I was in shock and worried her injuries might be more severe than I could see underneath her fur. Reports were filed, animal control informed me of my rights, and I was free to take myself to urgent care to receive a tetanus shot and have my wounds cleaned and bandaged. Animal control found out from the owner that the dog got out because his daughter left the gate open.

The week following the attack was filled with stressful vet visits, sleepless nights, bursts of crying and irrational anger, inability to focus or work, therapy sessions, and the torture of waiting for the quarantine period to end. If for some reason the dog turned out to have rabies, I would require expensive shots so I wouldn't get rabies. I neither wanted these shots nor wanted to die of rabies, so waiting to hear was paralyzing. During my days, I spent hours on the internet, looking up information regarding dog bites, pit bulls, rabies, infections, legal procedures, and insurance.

I'm unsure about the benefits of this behavior. My efforts failed to calm my fears and may have even increased them.

My husband and incredible friends were there for me in every way: coming to stay with me a few hours the night of the attack, watching my dog while I went to urgent care, responding swiftly and graciously to my numerous texts and crying phone calls. My closest friends were empathetic and helpful in every way, even crying with me or getting angry on my behalf. There is healing power in having someone outraged on your behalf. My close friends shined during a crisis. My dog continued to heal and got back to full-playing-strength. This lifted my spirits more than anything.

As I thought about everything that happened, one particular comment kept surfacing. It caused me to consider that maybe God himself saved my dog from death that day. Every single person I came in contact with, the urgent care doctor, the neighbor, the fireman, and the man in the waiting room at the vet said, "That's so crazy, because pit bulls don't usually release their jaws once they've bitten." No other dog possesses the pit bull's tenacity combined with their hold-and-shake bite style. They simply don't let go. Apparently it's controversial whether or not they have an actual locking jaw mechanism, but it seemed widely known that this breed differs from other breeds in their locking-on type of bite. Their attacks have been compared to shark attacks. I have now seen and heard enough stories to know that my dog surviving this attack was absolutely a miracle.

Why had this pit bull released, not once but twice? I had fallen to my knees and cried out for God to help me. But I did so in desperation, not in faith. I had simply hoped I would be heard and that God would intervene. I didn't know. I still wrestle with this thought and with my faith about intervention. I do choose to believe, based on all the evidence and everything I know, that God released the pit bull's jaws that day and spared my dog. I'm not sure I would have been the same if I witnessed my dog die in my arms.

As far as it depended on me, my dog wasn't going to die on my watch. But I couldn't save her, no matter how hard I tried. I believe God had mercy on me that day. He saved her when I couldn't.

Every day it gets a little easier to walk in our neighborhood. Every day I hear her screaming less and less. Every day the image of that dog on her neck fades away. But every day my certainty about what happened fades too, and I'm forced to decide what I believe. Did God intervene? Does he still perform miracles today? Who am I to say he doesn't? I don't know how or why he chooses to save some dogs and not others. I don't understand why some dogs get run over or killed in an attack like this and some don't. To take it even further, I don't understand why he chooses to heal some people and not others, to save some people from drowning, or dying in a car wreck, or in their sleep. These are the hardest questions I have, and they can make me doubt the goodness of God. It doesn't make any sense or seem fair. My mind cannot understand or explain the ways of God. But I know one thing: my dog was saved that January afternoon, and it wasn't my faith or strength that saved her, it was his.

29

CHURCH: WHY I STILL GO

I'm not alone in having mixed feelings about church. Whether you've been raised in the church or not, or as in my case, *especially* if you've been raised in church, the word "church" conjures complicated emotions. I don't know where you land on the spectrum, but if you still have a small desire to be a part of something sacred, maybe this will help. I have every reason to never want to set foot in church again, but I've worked it out, and I'm back.

Whether you consider yourself religious, spiritual, or neither, we all need a place to stop and rest and think about the mystery of life. For me that place is often somewhere near the ocean, but I can also be found in the pews or in someone's home gathering. Almost every week, I get myself out of the house, and of my own free will go to a place called church. I've got solid, grown-up, non-coerced reasons for going now, and that's made all the difference.

I was brought up in the church—sort of. My mother sent me to the local Baptist church by way of the church van that came around and picked up the kids each Sunday morning. She may have joined me a time or two, but mostly I went alone. My father certainly made us all go to church as long as we were "living under his roof." But Sunday was not a restful, peaceful day growing up in my father's house. We were always rushing and always late. My father was usually angry, and my stepmother didn't want to go any more than the kids did. When we got to church, we were either bored or terrified, depending on the message.

Fortunately, my experience with church changed when I was sixteen and started going to Key Biscayne Presbyterian Church. I had never been to a church like this before. I met people who had spiritual life in them—light seemed to show in their eyes. I felt cared for in a non-pushy way (they were Presbyterians after all; they don't like to push). I also began to listen to the sermons without fear hindering me. I heard about truth and grace, and for the first time began to understand things like the sovereignty of God and his unconditional love for all people.

Our pastor was Steve Brown, now a radio broadcaster, semi-nary professor, and published author of many books (all of which I highly recommend). Steve likes to say he's about making sure Christians know God isn't mad at them. That's exactly how I experienced Steve and Key Biscayne Presbyterian Church, the first place I came to hear about God and find out he wasn't mad at me.

At sixteen, I was a lost teenager from a broken home. I was looking for a safe place for the time between school and home, a place I could be myself and not be judged, where maybe I could even be liked. Their youth group became that place for me. We had an awesome youth pastor, which I know lots of people say about their youth pastor, but ours really was. I've met a lot of pastors and youth pastors since then, and I look back wondering how we got so lucky with Steve and Kent.

It may seem like a small thing, but Kent came to my high school graduation. He had many to attend, but he came to mine too, and that meant more than I can say. A lot of people were sentimental at graduation—families all around and pictures being taken. I felt like I was watching the whole thing from outside my body; I didn't feel anything except the awkwardness of the obligatory congratulations being doled out. Then Kent showed up, and I burst into tears. Someone cared that I existed, someone who wasn't obligated to be there. I'll never forget that.

Before Key Biscayne Presbyterian, we went to all kinds of churches—Baptist, Presbyterian, Messianic, and nondenominational. By the time I went to college, I had a smorgasbord of denominations to choose from. My first year of college, I simply went to chapel. It was a private, Christian college so we were required to go. I occasionally attended the big church associated with the college, but less and less by the time my sophomore year rolled around.

Until I was twenty-five, I floated from congregation to congregation, nothing really sticking. I kept comparing every church to Key Biscayne, and nothing measured up to Steve's teaching or the feeling I had as a member of Kent's youth group. My college friend, Phillip, was the son of a pastor at a local Lutheran Apostolic Church. I really liked him and his family, so I started going there. That was the first church that felt close to Key Biscayne. The teaching was great—bold and grace-filled. I felt like I belonged and like I had found a loving family.

Still, I was restless and moved around to other churches. Over the next few years, I was part of several churches and a variety of denominations, including Presbyterian, Episcopal, Charismatic, Lutheran, and Catholic. I finally landed in one place for a while and attended Center Point, a Presbyterian church in Tallahassee, for almost eight years—the longest I'd been at any church. I made some great friends there who remain some of my best friends to this day. I experienced community there—the kind where you meet regularly and share life and pray honest prayers together. Many of us haven't experienced community like that since. It was a special season in our lives. I left that church because I moved out of state. Otherwise I'd probably still be going there today.

Moving to Texas and looking for a church was a whole other

animal. Despite being in the Bible Belt with churches on every corner, searching for a new church my husband and I both agreed on was a challenge, to say the least. We tried going to his Messianic church. I lasted a year. We tried Presbyterian churches and Brethren churches and nondenominational churches. We quit going to a traditional church altogether and tried a "home group church," where we hosted church in our home as well as going to others' homes. We tried everything.

One of the better experiences occurred in the home group led by one of the pastors at a Presbyterian church we attended for a while. Their church was going through a difficult time, and the pastor and his wife were personally, deeply discouraged. We loved them and wanted to support them and needed support and community ourselves. The group was only about eight to ten people. We met in the pastor's home. He had an old piano in the living room and would often play hymns we'd sing along to. We tried reading Dietrich Bonhoeffer's book *Life Together*, but mostly we talked, prayed, and cried. We carried each other's burdens, cared enough to listen, prayed, and confessed to each other our struggles and joys. It was one of the best experiences of living in community I've ever been a part of. I call this real church. It's been hard to reproduce. It is a rare and sweet gift when you have it.

My husband travels 90 percent of the year for work, so I often go to church by myself. I started going to St. Andrews, a little Episcopal church around the corner from our house in McKinney. It's a Scripture-based church with little pretense and a wonderful, warm spirit. Both of the priests are humble and genuine, and each week I left church with the same feelings: no judgment, no pretense, and no agenda. They are gracious and loving people trying to follow Christ. They sing the old hymns, which I always love. I'm easily distracted, so I've never been comfortable in a huge church with a loud band, purple lights, and large video screens. For me, that's too much going on at once. For that reason and others, I like the simplicity of the hymns and simple worship. I am thankful for St.

Andrews. I'm still looking for a similar church in my new hometown in Florida. I need a place I can gather with sincere and kind people who have open hearts and listening ears.

During one of the sermons at St. Andrews I heard words that rarely, if ever, come from the pulpit (or from any Christian, for that matter). It was during a time when hate speech from religious people was abounding against homosexuality. Instead of sidestepping the issue, the head priest got up and said, "On behalf of the church, I apologize for the things said and done in the name of Christ that were not what God intended. Christ loves all people." It was a powerful and holy moment; one I wish weren't so rare. If people heard statements like this regularly, maybe one day Christians could be known for their extreme humility and love more than their judgment.

The location, the pastors and priests, and the buildings will change, but I'll still keep going to church as long as I live. Church is in me; church is a part of me. I believe I am the church, and you are the church, and like the Scripture says: *"For where two or three are gathered together in my name, there am I in the midst of them"* (Matthew 18:20, KJV). I don't believe the place we gather is the best definition of the church, but we don't have to agree on this point to be friends. After my long journey through different types of churches, I still go to a place called church.

I go to acknowledge there's someone greater than me.

I go to bend a knee and submit myself to that someone.

I go to be with people who are saying, "I don't know it all, I need help to find the truth, I need mercy, I need grace, I need wisdom."

I go to be with God, who is everywhere and in everything all the time, especially other people who love him.

I go to quiet my soul from all the noise in the world and in me.

I go to listen.

I go to be still.

I go to pray.

I go to cry.
I go to sing.
I go for peace.
I go for faith.
I go for hope.
I go for love.

30

PRAYER AND THE BIBLE:
MYSTERIOUS GIFTS

I have more questions than answers when it comes to some of the gifts God has given his people. For two in particular—prayer and the Bible—I don't have answers, but I have honesty, I have my story, and I have hope in the giver of these gifts.

Prayer

I've always struggled with prayer. I've rarely seen it modeled in a way I want to emulate. Some people do crazy things with prayer. The only prayers I've heard by others that seemed honest contained few, simple words. The more people say when praying, the more I feel that they begin to sound like they're orating and enjoying the sound of their own voices. Additionally, making lists of people to pray for seems awkward and forced to me. I end up feeling mechanical going down my list. The acronym prayers, such as ACTS (adoration, confession, thanksgiving, supplication) are helpful guides. But those too feel mechanical after a while. Prayer is hard, but maybe it doesn't have to be. Maybe I'm making it too difficult. Maybe it's mysterious for a reason.

A few kinds of prayer don't leave me feeling like a religious robot. I appreciate the *Book of Common Prayer* in this way. I feel comforted and guided by the prayers it contains. When I don't know what to pray but have the desire to pray, these liturgical prayers give me the words I'm looking for but can't seem to find. They also connect me to people of faith who lived hundreds of years before me and prayed the same prayers. Praying the Psalms has the same effect.

I also have been trying to turn my anxious thoughts and worries into prayers. If I am worried about a particular person, these types of thoughts can be simple prayers. *God, help them and be with them.* If I'm feeling anxious and worried myself, I might think or pray silently, *God, help me to let this go. Help me to trust you with it and stop thinking about it so much.* Simple-minded to some, but for me it is honest and genuine. I think God wants our honesty more than anything.

The Psalms reveal honest emotions. This book in the Bible is filled with questions, struggles, and a wide range of emotions. It's also filled with promises. One of the raw, honest songs I have used regularly when anxious is this one:

> *Quiet my mind Lord, make me still before you. Calm my restless heart Lord, make me more like you. Raise up my hands that are hanging down, strengthen my feeble knees. May your love and grace abound and fill me with your peace.*

Simple, humble, powerful.

Praying doesn't make me feel more important or more spiritual. Praying the Psalms or reciting from the *Book of Common Prayer* doesn't make me feel religious—it makes me feel human. It also makes me feel my humanity and my need for the divine. I need God. I need his presence in my life. I need other people around me who know they need of God too.

Prayer is mysterious. I don't understand it. I don't always know what I'm doing. But if I give up trying, I give up a gift. Something happens to my mind and soul when I pray and get quiet and still: I receive the gift of peace. When I drown out all the chatter and noise of the world and focus on the person of Christ, I am as at peace as I can ever be in this life.

The Bible

The first thing I had to do as an adult trying to read the Scriptures was recover from being mentally beaten with the Bible. My reading of the Bible is in constant tension with my history and experience. I do believe it is the inspired and inerrant word of God, the source of all truth, and the foundation of my faith. However, the memories and feelings I have associated with the Bible plague me daily. They compete with my desire to be guided by the Scriptures in everything I do. I am at war with the past while I try to move into a healthier future.

I was brought up in fundamentalist churches, what I know as the birthplace of "Bible beatings." Sermons weren't Spirit-filled messages of hope, love, and forgiveness. They were dominated by sweaty, screaming preachers calling for repentance or proclaiming eternal damnation. When the messages weren't directly about repentance, there was still a tone of condemnation that accompanied each sermon and the verses attached to them. Maybe it was just the tradition, maybe it was just certain churches, or maybe it was just my imagination. But I don't know how a child could imagine such things.

As a child, I was curious and open to what I was being taught in church. I was still hopeful and innocent and ready to believe. Yet three main themes were on auto repeat on Sundays and dominated my childhood understanding of the Bible:

You are a filthy, rotten sinner with all kinds of evil flowing through your body.

You need to repent of your sins and evil ways immediately because Jesus could come back at any time and you wouldn't want to be left behind.

You need to accept Jesus into your heart as Lord and Savior. And if you have done it before, you need to be *sure* you meant it, otherwise you might not be saved. It is best to do it again to be certain, and while you're at it, rededicate your life to following the Lord if you have strayed from the path.

You may think I am exaggerating, but I assure you I'm not. These themes were as present as the gold offering plates and the weekly altar calls. The tricky thing is, there's good about these messages, in part. I believe I was born with a sinful nature and am in need of redemption. I also believe I need to repent of my sins and follow Christ. I have asked Jesus to save me and help me follow him and live a life of love. If you're not from a Christian background, I know that all these words sound weird and unnatural. I am from a Christian background, and they still sound that way to me. To put it another way, I believe in God, the creator and sustainer of the universe. I believe in Christ and that he was the Son of God, sent to save mankind from a life separated from God. I believe in the Holy Spirit who is present with me. And I believe the Bible is the source of all this truth.

I've always been confused by my old churches' venomous communication about my sinful state. Wasn't it enough to know that I was in need? Was it made truer if I felt shame and humiliation by being regularly and repeatedly referred to as a dirty, rotten sinner, instead of a child of God in need of him?

I don't know where these types of preachers get their direction and instruction, but I don't think it is from a correct interpretation of the Bible. They instill fear about one's faith not being sincere enough; where does that idea come from? According to the Scriptures, when did your request for God to save you, fail? There were many times I was terrified to the point where I constantly questioned myself and repeated the same prayer over and over again, trying to gain some assurance or certainty. Is this the life of faith and trust the Bible speaks of? Is this what God had in mind when, in love, he called us to himself for life and salvation? I don't think so.

If the Bible was used against us, that understandably shapes how we think and feel about it. For example, when I was in high school and my father found out I was sleeping with my boyfriend, part of my punishment was to memorize Psalm 51 in its entirety. Now mind you, this is a beautiful, inspired Psalm with rich meaning. However, when your father, who you are sure hates you and is disgusted with you, gives you a chapter of the Bible to memorize instead of talking with you about it, you believe the Bible itself is the punishment. The Bible was only used to tell me how bad I was. So for me there was always a direct correlation between the Bible and my sinfulness. For most of my life, I only associated the Bible with punishment.

I have spent the last twenty-five years trying to unlearn what I thought the Bible was saying. I am convinced that how I was taught the Bible was the problem, not the Bible itself. I am not a theologian or a Bible scholar. I don't think you have to be to read the Bible. I am a flawed human trying to find an honest faith, and I believe the Bible is central to that faith. I need help to understand the Bible in the way God intended it. I think that help comes in many forms. The Bible says something about the Spirit helping us. I believe that. I've also witnessed some honest, humble, and thoughtful scholars, pastors, priests, and regular people explain their take on what the Bible says. Those are the explanations I trust the most, especially when they are willing to say they could be wrong.

The Bible is a mystery to me. I don't think God made it a

mystery to toy with us, but I don't know why he wrote it the way he did. Yet I am glad there is something mysterious to turn to for wisdom, inspiration, and grace. I wouldn't want to live in a world without this gift. I also have much more to learn about the God who wrote this book through ordinary people. I have a suspicion he is quite different from what I have believed. I am curious to find out.

31

QUIET RETREATING: THE POWER OF SILENCE, STILLNESS, AND SAFE FRIENDS

I'm not sure when I first began to love the quiet. It might have been when I was about four. Quiet places represented safety. It might have been in college, when the only quiet I found was at the campus library. Maybe it was the smell of books or the clean, defined spaces, but I liked the feeling of being with people without having to talk. I felt lost in college, never sure about my purpose. Getting a degree was obviously the goal, but it didn't give me a sense of purpose. When I was at the library, I could enjoy a temporary sense of purpose; I was there to study for an exam or write a paper. The purpose of my existence in that moment was clear. I enjoyed the purpose—and the quiet.

An experience I had while on a spiritual renewal retreat in my late twenties cemented my love for the quiet. A friend told me about a retreat called Tres Dias, meaning three days. It was an ecumenical group, a bunch of Christians of all denominations. The purpose of these retreats was to help Christians become closer to God.

During one of the evenings after a chapel meeting and dinner, we were instructed to return to our cabins in silence and to remain silent for the rest of the evening. You can imagine how difficult this was for a group of women sharing close quarters. I'd never experienced anything like this before and was surprised by how much I liked it. With each hour that passed, I felt more relaxed and peaceful. The pressure to talk with strangers was gone. The pressure to make conversation, even with people I knew, was lifted. I could simply be there with no expectation other than to be quiet with my own thoughts. I loved this unexpected gift.

A few years later, in my early thirties, I decided I wanted to recreate this experience with a few of my close friends. I didn't know exactly what it would look like, or what we would do other than be quiet, but I knew we could start there. A few friends had been meeting together regularly for years for book clubs and Bible studies. We were all different personalities, but had one thing in common: we wanted to become more like Christ. I wasn't sure how they would respond to my suggestion of being quiet, or if they would enjoy it as I had. But I wanted to be a part of giving this gift to others, if they wanted it.

My idea was similar to what would happen at a silent retreat. These are spiritual retreats where groups or individuals go into the wilderness, with no TV, computers, or phones, and speak to no one for days. My version is a little different. Silence in the wilderness for days was not appealing to me. However, a quiet atmosphere in cabins by the river, with food and air conditioning, sounded delightful. We would disconnect from electronics, work, and society, but we would still be together. We wouldn't talk, but we would have the comfort of each other's presence as we ate, drank, read, wrote, prayed, and rested.

I thought three or four of us could go on an overnight retreat and try being silent for twenty-four hours. I found a retreat center less than an hour away. It was on the Suwannee River in North Florida, and it was idyllic. They had inexpensive rooms available in an inn-like setting, with wooden rocking chairs on the porches overlooking the river. There were plenty of places to walk on trails or around the campgrounds. There was even a little homestyle diner right downstairs where we could buy breakfast, lunch, and dinner. There were small conference rooms and large living rooms with fireplaces and comfy couches. It was perfect. I provided excerpts from my favorite devotional writers, Scripture, the Book of Common Prayer, other meditations, poems, or journaling exercises. The topics were always centered on spiritual renewal.

For the last eighteen years, once a year, a group of friends have gathered for these retreats. Some years we had them at hotels and resorts, some years on the river. Our favorite place is the beach. We like to do it right and find a luxury beach house with all the accommodations, bring the best food and wine, and really settle in for a few days. Of course this isn't necessary; any quiet location out of town will do. I've found the essential elements to be quiet and safety—the rest is up to you.

Something happens to the soul when you get quiet and still. At first it can be unnerving and the mind is anything but quiet. After a while, though, it calms down and your thoughts can become clear and peaceful. Everybody's experience is different, but the benefits of the time away from responsibilities, electronics, and the demands of life are always felt and treasured. In the beginning, I would go on these weekends with an agenda for ways I wanted healing or answered prayers. I quickly learned this was not happening. I had a bad habit of demanding God do things in my way and in my time. The more of an agenda I had, the more resistance I felt. A better way surfaced: show up, be quiet, be still, meditate on true words, eat when you're hungry, rest when you're tired, and receive whatever comes.

These retreats are essential in my life. They restore my focus and balance. They remind me of what's important. Frederick Buechner says in his book *Secrets in the Dark*:

> Part of the inner world of everyone is this sense of emptiness, unease, incompleteness, and I believe that this in itself is a word

from God, that this is the sound that God's voice makes in a world that has explained him away. In such a world, I suspect that maybe God speaks to us most clearly through his silence, his absence, so that we know him best through our missing him.[1]

Going on these retreats with close friends who have the same goals and desires in mind is also part of the way I live in community. I don't flourish on my own; I need people. I suppose technically you could do these retreats on your own. Personally, I have tried and it doesn't work for me. Something about being among friends, all there for the same purpose, helps keep my mind from wandering and keeps me focused on why I'm there in the first place.

Safe, healthy friends are a gift. Sharing this kind of life with them doubles the benefits. Henri Nouwen says it better than I can:

> A friend can be that person with whom we can share our solitude, our silence, and our prayer. A friend can be that person with whom we can look at a tree and say, "Isn't that beautiful?" or sit on the beach and silently watch the sun disappear under the horizon. With a friend we don't have to say or do something special. With a friend we can be still and know that God is there with both of us.[2]

32

THREE THINGS I WISH CHRISTIANS WOULD SAY MORE

Christians are not widely known for their love for people. This is sad, disappointing, and frustrating. We are supposed to be people recognized as followers of Christ based on our love for each other. Sadly, historically and today, nothing seems further from the truth. If you asked a hundred people what word came to mind when you said the word Christian, I bet the number one word would be "judgmental." We love to judge people; it's in our DNA. We also love to be right, we love certainty, and we love helping ourselves more than we help others. That's a far cry from being known by our love. I am a part of this problem. I would like to change and become part of a solution. I'm tired of being identified with a faith that is known more for being hateful, self-righteous, and hypocritical. I've chosen three phrases we could increasingly add to our speech that might help. They are: I don't know for sure, I'm sorry, and how can I help?

I Don't Know for Sure

Certainty and self-righteousness abound in Christian culture. We love to be right and we love to tell others how right we are, especially when it comes to religion and morality. We are not comfortable with loose ends, doubt, and mystery. We want to definitively know the answers to things. But what would be the harm in simply saying, "I believe this means this or that, but I don't know for sure." We like to be the authority on subjects, especially those that make us feel powerful. And what better subject to feel powerful and certain about than religion? I don't know about you, but religion has made me feel more powerless than most things in my life. The more I learn, the less certain I am. The things I feel certain about still require a measure of faith and allow for mystery and doubt. I feel certain God exists, that he loves me and everyone who's ever lived and ever will live, and that he gave us Christ who made spiritual life possible again. Beyond that, I am not 100 percent certain about anything, and I am weary of people who claim to be. To say we don't know for sure is to say we are not God. To me, not knowing for sure simply means I still have more to learn and I am listening.

We love to talk. Listening doesn't seem to be as appealing. TV talk shows, radio talk shows, news talk shows, podcasts, seminars, conferences, and tours abound. We love to spout our ideas about everything: politics, sexuality, and religion. Everybody has something to say.

Whenever I'm in a group of people, I like to look for the people who don't appear to be talking as much as others. I've discovered it's not because they have nothing to say, but because they are gathering information and thinking before they speak. Sometimes it's the people who want to be the center of attention that I have the most trouble listening to. I haven't always been a great listener, but I'm getting better. I want to hear what other people have to say instead of just waiting for my turn to talk again—that's not listening.

How about saying, "I don't know for sure" when talking about suffering? Especially when people are hurting, we want so badly to give answers and make them feel better. But it doesn't help to say things we don't actually know like, "It will get better in time." Will it? What if it's the loss of a child? Wouldn't that always hurt in some way? The most common phrase I hear is "at least." "At least such-and-such didn't happen." Or some variation of "it could be worse." We say these things because we hope they will encourage and offer perspective. But I've never been encouraged by these words; in fact, they usually make me feel worse. People who say these things are well-meaning, I have no doubt, but I have never met someone who felt better after hearing such comments. When you're a kid, the worst phrase is "it builds character." As an adult, I still hear this, mostly from Christians: "This pain and suffering you're going through is such a great opportunity for growth." Yes, yes it is. But please don't say that. Please, for now, just listen to me and be with me.

I'm Sorry

Sometimes we say true things to people with pure and empathetic intentions. But even then it may be best not to speak at all. What if all they need is to feel the pain of the situation, so they can move through it and beyond it? What if sitting with them while they hurt is the comfort they need most? What if we are doing more harm than good with our words and good intentions? What if the best thing we can do for people in pain is to sit quietly with them and listen?

I've learned that being quiet and listening empathetically is sometimes the best choice. Saying, "I'm sorry" is second only to that. And I don't mean the quick, insincere version. There are many reasons to say I'm sorry. I say it when I'm wrong, when I've hurt someone, and when they've told me something painful that's happened to them. I mentioned earlier how one of my pastors apologized on behalf of the church for things said and done in the name of Christ that were not what he intended. This type of humble apology is the one I am most thankful for. I want to be a person who is quick to forgive and be forgiven and someone who is quick to listen and slow to answer. This seems like a good place to start.

How Can I Help?

One of the ways we can counteract our tendency to judge people we disagree with is to ask, "How can I help?" We have to listen to find out the real need, and we have to lay down our judgment if we want to serve. It is harder to judge someone when you see his or her need. If we want to be known as people who love, we will serve people more. And not just those we find it easy to serve, but those we have nothing in common with, those we disagree with, and even those we may dislike. Love is not only a feeling. Love is an action.

Our world is often a cold, dark, harsh place to live. To be a Christian in this world, we have to break through that darkness with love, and I personally don't see that happening nearly often enough. Until the day comes when we are truly known by our love, we can't stop asking important questions.

I need to say when I'm wrong. I need to ask for and receive forgiveness. I need to say when I don't know something for sure. I need to say I'm sorry for the horrible things happening to people in this world. And I need to help people because of how much I've been helped.

33

WHERE IS THE HAPPY ENDING?

So what's the point? What's the bottom line? Why tell all the sad stories? Why tell stories at all? And where is the happy ending? The happy ending is . . . I am alive! I found some joy. I have some peace, and more—so much more—is coming. The point is I didn't die from my wounds, I won't die for my sins, and I won't die without knowing I have been loved and have loved in return. To me, there is nothing greater than this—to know, really know, love and forgiveness.

There is still much work to do in the world. But I won't do any of it very well without knowing the answer to the one question every single person on the planet is asking: Am I loved? I believe the answer God gives is YES—unequivocally, unconditionally, and everlastingly. After everything I've seen and all I've been through, I can finally say that I really believe this, even if imperfectly.

As an adult, I have taken the things that happened to me as a child—things that turned a trusting child into a cynic—held them up to God, and asked why and for what purpose. He has given no direct answers, only hints and possibilities. I would like to know more, even now. For most of my life, not knowing why those things happened made me angry. But over time I began to experience some relief from questioning and struggling and began to see glimpses of light and hope. God began to show me that my life wasn't a waste and the pain wasn't for nothing. He showed me this through others, through their honest way of living and their kindness to me. I met Christians who seemed filled with light. I believed them when they spoke. They told the truth. They had no agenda. They asked nothing of me. They just loved me. They listened to me, they spent time with me, they invited me into their homes, they shared meals with me, they let me take care of their children, they laughed with me when things were funny, and they cried with me when things were sad. They seemed to care about my life. They seemed to care I existed. This was the way I learned about God. This was the way I was slowly healed. Not with answers, but with love. In this way, God loved me through others doing the very thing I needed God to do the most, *be with me*. I can handle anything if I know God is with me.

I still question God sometimes. I still have many of the same questions everybody has: Why do bad things have to happen at all? If God is good and God is love, why do we have so much suffering? God continues to answer me the same way he always has: with love. I have not believed him, not trusted him, and not been grateful. Yet still he loves me. Maybe this is the best evidence of all that God is good.

I still struggle to believe and trust at times. I think I always will. This is where my brokenness is most evident: I am hardwired not to trust. I've been taught that trusting is a bad idea. But that isn't the whole story. I am learning to trust. I realize that I have valid reasons for not being quick to trust others, but I also know that if I never get any better at trusting, I am still loved, and that thought alone transforms my broken heart.

Many people with my history don't end up with the wonderful, full life I have now. It's not without struggles, but it's so much better than I deserve. I could have gotten pregnant multiple times outside of marriage. I could have been a single mom. I could have married a womanizer, been in a loveless marriage, or gotten divorced multiple times. I could have become a drug addict, ended up in jail, or landed in a psychiatric hospital. I could have never been financially stable and debt-free. I could have never been in a loving marriage, never been able to be a loving stepmom or loving friend to my friend's children. I could have missed out on healthy community, church, and loving friends. I could have never wanted to set foot in church again or believed in God at all.

But that didn't happen. And it wasn't because I made great decisions and pulled it all together. It began with the mercy of God in my life. Yes, I made some good decisions and worked for my current health. But I made many, many poor decisions as well. There is no way I should have the life I have now. I cannot and do not take credit for it. It was by the grace of God that I was ever able to make the first good choice, and the grace of God for every good choice after that.

So what's the point of telling the stories? People are the point; people and their hearts. They are the most important part of any good story. We need to know we are not alone, especially in our pain. We all have some version of these stories, and they matter. My life and the lives of countless others matter. We are all living under the weight of these stories until they are told. We grow weary under that weight. I write for these people as much or more than I write for myself.

I remain a curious mixture of hope and sadness, light and darkness, and I will be as long as I'm living. But one day I'll live in the new heavens and new earth—finally at home with God. I'll have complete joy and perfect peace. No more darkness, only light. Until then, I live in the in-between, in the shadows and in the sun. I'll be waiting for that day when there's no more sorrow and no more tears. Until then, I remain ever light and dark.

ENDNOTES

Chapter 11, Being Single

1. Patrick, Darren, and Candace Bushnell, writers "Where There's Smoke..." In *Sex and the City*, directed by Michael Patrick King. HBO. June 4, 2000.

Chapter 14, Mother

1. Remnant, in *Dictionary.com*, https://www.dictionary.com/browse/remnant.

Chapter 17: Friends

1. Thomas Merton, The Seven Storey Mountain, 50th anniversary ed. (Orlando: Hartcourt Inc., 1992), 62.
2. Henri Nouwen, Life of the Beloved (New York: Crossroad Publishing, 1992).

Chapter 19: Being Married

1. *To the Wonder*, written and directed by Terrence Malick, 2012.

Chapter 24: Counseling

1. "Non-clinical Depression," *DepressionFree.com*, last updated October 3, 2018. http://www.depressionfree.com/non-clinical.html.

2. *Postcards from the Edge*, directed by Mike Nichols (1990, Los Angeles, CA: Sony Movie Channel, 2001), DVD.

Chapter 31: Quiet Retreating

1. Fredrick Buechner, *Secrets in the Dark: A Life in Sermons* (San Francisco: HarperSanFrancisco, 2006), 19.

2. Henri Nouwen, Bread for the Journey: A Daybook of Wisdom and Faith (New York: HarperOne, 1997).

ABOUT THE AUTHOR

Elizabeth lives in Ponte Vedra Beach, Florida, with her husband, Tim, and sweet dog, Hoolah. She graduated from Florida State University and worked more than twenty years in the legal field before working five years in the nonprofit world. She believes that any day connecting with real friends in real time is a good, good day.

Me, three years old

My parents

My sister Jen

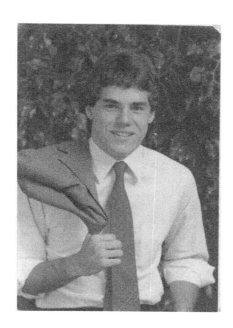

My brother Michael

Getting ready for church

The Miller kids

My Stepmom and sister Melissa

My Father and Bryan

My brother Bryan

Tim and me

facebook.com/elizabeth.m.hayes.1

instagram.com/elizabeth.m.hayes.1

Made in the USA
Coppell, TX
20 February 2020

16039259R00125